HOW TO WORK WITH AN
INTERIOR DESIGNER

HOW TO WORK WITH AN INTERIOR DESIGNER

JUDY SHERIDAN, ASID, CID

Gibbs Smith, Publisher

TO ENRICH AND INSPIRE HUMANKIND

Salt Lake City | *Charleston* | *Santa Fe* | *Santa Barbara*

To Ellen L. Vanook

First Edition
12 11 10 09 08   5 4 3 2 1
Text © 2008 Judy Sheridan
Photography copyrights as noted throughout

Published by
Gibbs Smith, Publisher
P.O. Box 667
Layton, Utah 84041

Orders: 1.800.835.4993
www.gibbs-smith.com

Designed by Black Eye Design
Printed and bound in China

Library of Congress Cataloging-in-Publication Data
Sheridan, Judy.
  How to work with an interior designer / Judy Sheridan.— 1st ed.
      p. cm.
  ISBN-13: 978-1-4236-0195-1
  ISBN-10: 1-4236-0195-5
  1. Interior decoration—Handbooks, manuals, etc. I. Title.
  NK2115.S476 2008
  747—dc22
                              2007048220

Contents

The idea to write a book on how to work with an interior designer originated with my publisher, Gibbs Smith. My two other published books had been about window treatment design and easy decorating ideas, so the suggestion to write about a profession very dear to my heart was intriguing. The more I thought about the experiences I had had working for other interior designers, running my own business, and dealing with clients, the more I thought the book was necessary and timely.

I saw my impending tenure as president of the New York Metropolitan Chapter of the American Society of Interior Designers (ASID) as an opportunity to gain a broader look at this profession and, in turn, to have expanded contact with an association of other interior designers. Add to this scenario the ever-growing popularity of television shows on interior design, a genre which fosters, in my opinion, an unrealistic view of what it is like to design, install, and finish an interior design project. These programs, however, have had a positive side effect: they have produced a dramatic surge in the interest and popularity in interior design. Now, more than ever, people are working with interior designers, AND they know what interior design is. However, I realized that something was still missing: a basic and thorough understanding of the interior design process and the role of the interior designer. At this point I realized I had something to say.

It seemed to me that to detail what it's like to work with an interior designer on a project and follow the design process would benefit everyone . . . client and designer. It would clarify a lot of the mystery about design. It would also debunk many of the myths about design procedures and misconceptions about the designer. It would enable both client and designer to work together in greater harmony, as the client would now have a better understanding of the design process and an increased appreciation for all that the interior designer does. I want your experience of working with an interior designer to be as enjoyable and rewarding as it can possibly be.

Judy Sheridan
Sheridan Interiors, Inc.
January 2008

Foreword

Lights, camera, action! From her starlet years to today, Judy Sheridan knows how to get things done in a highly stylish and effective way. This whirling design dervish has the energy, smarts, and style to create interior magic for her clients and now the readers of *How to Work with an Interior Designer*. Judy's first career in the world of theatre prepared her to be the ultimate optimist, leading her to become an expert on raising the curtain on perfect interiors. From the initial audition right through to the opening night raves, *How to Work with an Interior Designer* is a primer on how to work with a professional interior designer.

I have relied on Judy's wisdom, guidance, and knowledge for many years. With a gift for sharing, she now imparts her sagacity to the world. Starting with the basic question of why you need a designer and clearly explaining the benefits a designer brings to a project, Judy guides the reader through every step of the process, all the way to project completion. Demystifying the oft-closed world of design, she explains clearly and succinctly the various aspects of the process of working with a design pro. Essential chapters on selecting a designer, understanding the fee schedules, defining your project, establishing a budget, and tracking the project in process are included. Judy has even anticipated the ever-present challenge of what to do when something goes awry and suggests resolution steps to the inevitable problem, taking the scare factor out of the equation.

Judy's exquisite eye and attention to detail is legend among design aficionados and her clients. Now she brings the same finesse that animates her famous interior confections to this topic. Like one of her famous, perfectly draped swag-and-jabot window treatments, adorned with braid trim over beaded fringe, *How to Work with an Interior Designer* makes the decision to partner with an interior designer effortless. Judy Sheridan has shared her encyclopedic experience in this book, and, by the end, it is clear that the perfect throw pillow on the perfect sofa awaits the reader in the perfect room. Lean back, relax, and savor the experience.

Jamie Drake
Drake Design Associates
January 2008

Acknowledgments

I would like to acknowledge the following people for their kindness and generosity in offering me guidance, their own experiences, photographs of interior design projects, and, most especially, encouragement. In short, whatever I asked of them, they gave and they gave unstintingly. For this, I am eternally indebted to the following interior designers and friends:

Clifford Atkinson, ASID; Diane Bianchini; Colleen Borek, Allied member ASID; Bob Buchanan; Dee Chenier, ASID; Maggie Cohen, ASID; Robin Conners; Jamie Drake, ASID; Judith M. Fox, ASID; Jamie Gibbs, Allied member ASID; Judy Girod, FASID; Alexander Goldstein, ASID; Phyllis Harbinger, ASID; Karen Hershman, Allied member ASID; Catherine Howard; Benjamin Huntington, ASID; David Kaplan, Allied member ASID; David Landy, ASID; Rocco Marianni; Shari Markbreiter, Allied member ASID; Charles Pavarini III, Allied member ASID; Beth Roeder, Allied member ASID; Esther Sadowsky, Allied member ASID; Irving Solero; Marshal Stearns; Terry Stewart, Allied member, ASID; Ché Swanson; Michelle Wenitsky, Allied member ASID; and Randy F. Wilson.

I am also grateful to the American Society of Interior Designers (ASID), for their generous permission in letting me use the Residential Interior Design Services Agreement form, and the National Council for Interior Design Qualification (NCIDQ), for their generous permission in letting me use excerpts from the practice analysis of the interior design process.

Thanks also to the following clients who—unknowingly at the time—provided the experiences that shaped and formed the basis for this book:

Nancy (Tex) Beha; Iris Cantor; John Desiderio; Janet and David Gochman; Dr. Stuart Grayson; Dr. Robert Haar; Jack and Veronica Kehoe; Arthur and Linda Leonard; Marla Muns; Laura and Jerry Nassau; James O'Hern; Nina O'Hern; Dr. Yvonne Rountree; Dr. Guillermo Seco; Morna and John Sheehy; Paula and Howard Slonim; Clifford Stevens; Kathryn L. Turner; Ellen L. Vanook; MaryAnn Van Osdal; Harold Varrah; Kathy Voehl; and Ralph and Myrna Yung.

Finally, I would like to express my gratitude to Leslie Stitt, my editor, for her talent and steadfast guidance that have made this book possible.

Introduction

This book describes what it's like to work with an interior designer and reveals some of the vastness of the very grand subject called Interior Design. It begins with the first thought you have about designing or redesigning a space. Next comes the decision to hire an interior designer, how to find the most appropriate person for your situation, and what to do, once you have made your choice, to get your project underway. It takes you through the various stages of what actually takes place during the course of designing a project—what to expect, what the designer does, what your role is—all the way through to completion. Think of it as the ABCs of an interior design project.

There has always been difficulty in understanding the design process. I suspect this is so because so much of what a designer does is cerebral. If you can't see the process, if it's not quantifiable, then somehow it is hard to define or to understand. Although the design process as it occurs in the designer is elusive, it is very understandable. Designers have an ability to see space, not as it is, but as it can be. Balance, proportion, and scale are a set of intangibles that gives the designer a seemingly extra-special sense of being able to envision a design. This may seem mysterious to many, but, to the designer, it's just how it is. The designer's ability to visualize space goes hand in hand with an amplified imagination for expression.

On the more practical side of design, this book covers the basics of how to determine when you need an interior designer and, of course, the benefits of having one. Other basics such as making the commitment to get started, having a budget (and staying within one), as well as managing your funds are reviewed. These are areas that most people are not terribly comfortable talking about, yet it is vital that these things be discussed and settled before you begin. You will certainly want to know the different ways that a designer has of working and which will be the best one for you.

It is important that you be prepared to deal with the many different phases that you will go through during the course of a project. You need to understand the documents that are part of a design project—a very critical subject—beginning with the agreement (contract) you have with the designer, followed by floor plans and design drawings, which, in turn, are followed by estimates or proposals for the products and services that you will order, and culminating with invoices and punch lists.

The period of designing your project and the various experiences you can expect to share with your designer, such as making design decisions and shopping, is where you will have exciting and challenging moments. You will also be meeting contractors, cabinetmakers, possibly architects or other professional consultants, and you need to have a good idea of who does what and what their areas of expertise are.

You need to know how to be prepared for when the work begins and what to do once it does. The period during which the work is performed will bring a variety of people into your life, and possibly problems as well. You will have lots of decisions to make. Knowing what to expect beforehand will help you deal with all of this confidently and more effectively.

Suggestions are offered for the times when things may not go smoothly, especially when differences of opinion occur—and they surely will. Options for handling matters of design, taste, and differing viewpoints are reviewed. Another important area to understand is the stages of the design development process. A step-by-step explanation gives you enough knowledge to see how a design project takes shape: how it goes from being an idea, to a design that becomes form, takes shape, is installed, all the way to the finished product—which is your beautifully designed space.

Sprinkled throughout the book are tips and words of advice that come from someone who admits that she is still learning everyday. Interior design is an ever-changing subject—there is always something new to discover—and as I continue to learn and grow in this profession, I am constantly reminded of how wondrous and stimulating it is.

To help you manage the learning process, there are sample documents, forms, and checklists in the Appendix, which will be useful in the course of your project.

When you are working with a designer, you are a special part of the design team. The sharing, the disagreements (let's face it—you will not agree all of the time), the camaraderie experienced when you "find" things, and the thrill of having a well-designed, finished space are all part of the adventure you have decided to undertake. You will discover new worlds along the way, and in the process you may find yourself with a whole new lifestyle.

Welcome to the fascinating world of Interior Design.

One

How can an interior designer help you? How do you know when to consider hiring an interior designer? What should you expect from an association with a designer? The answers to just these three questions can truly help you transform your lifestyle.

Lifestyle—your lifestyle—is how you choose to live and express yourself on a day-to-day basis. It begins with your home environment, extends to the way you dress, to what your choices are for cars, vacations, and pets, and, by extension, to your family members. I believe that life should be lived as smoothly, cleanly, and comfortably as possible. It begins with a home that truly makes you happy, where waking up in the morning and looking around the room is an invigorating experience. For most people, having an interior designer is the key to accomplishing this.

So why isn't everyone working with a designer? Several reasons that instantly come to mind are inertia, procrastination, and affordability. However, there are other issues that I think commonly prevent people from deciding to work with an interior designer.

Why People Don't Contact an Interior Designer

INDECISION

Indecision is a problem both for the client and the designer. Do you have a hard time making up your mind? Are there simply too many choices out there for you to pick "just one"? Or do you make up your mind quickly only to start vacillating about your choice later on?

If you are indecisive, clearly you are someone who should be working with an interior designer. For many people it is agonizing to have to make decisions—it is easier to keep putting them off. But let's say that you've actually taken the first step and you are determined to work with an interior designer. Chapter Three will deal with how to find the right designer for you and your project.

For a builder, an indecisive client prevents a project from moving ahead in a progressive fashion. When an indecisive customer waffles, everything goes on hold, interrupting the flow of the work, delaying the finish, and frequently adding to the cost of the job. Here is where an interior designer is invaluable. Your designer helps you focus on what needs to be decided, gives you advice and guidance in making a decision, and makes you aware of potential problems and additional costs if you change your mind later on.

If you are a chronically indecisive person, remind yourself that a decision is not forever. In your life it will be only one decision out of hundreds. This takes a lot of pressure off of having to make a "forever" decision. Tell yourself this is not

FACING: An elegantly appointed bedroom has an unusually high headboard with button tufting giving a "pillowed" effect—a quietly dramatic room. *Design: Roeder Design Group; photo © 2008 by Don Pearse Photographers, Inc.*

the only chance you will ever have to buy a sofa or a carpet, select a floor for a bathroom, or choose a fabric for a window treatment.

If you are confident in your designer's capabilities, you might want the designer to take over the decision-making process entirely. But, a word of caution: even if the designer is right on target

> If you are confident in your designer's capabilities, you might want the designer to take over the decision-making process entirely.

with your taste level, be sure that you are going to be comfortable with and prepared to live with someone else's choices.

DECISIVENESS

Maybe you have no trouble deciding what you want, and you look forward to making decisions. Perhaps you know exactly what you want your house to look like. Your concerns are that if you work with a professional you will have no say in what's going on, that he or she will take over, that your decisions will be ignored or challenged, or that you will wind up with a design that isn't what you want. You then decide you're probably better off working without a designer.

A designer is trained to *work with* you, to talk to you about your project, to respect your opinions, to make you aware of other options available to you, but also to advise you when your choices may not be the best ones. A relationship with a designer is a collaborative one, not one of superior and subordinate. You, in fact, are the best kind of client.

Few things make a job go more smoothly than clients who know what they want, make decisions easily, and want to get the job done. Sometimes, however, decisive clients can be inflexible, refusing to budge on decisions that should be reconsidered, or they are determined to be right at any cost. If that describes you, start being receptive to different ideas and suggestions. A successful relationship for an interior design project is not about any one person being

right, it is all about what looks best and what is right for you.

FINANCIAL CONCERNS

Does the thought of how much it's going to cost prevent you from calling a designer? Do you equate having a designer with that of making a major investment? Do you think that, no matter what is decided initially, a project will wind up costing much more than what you had budgeted?

I had a client once who, as we finished reviewing a sizable stack of proposals for his project, got up from the table and said that he suddenly felt a draft coming through the hole in his hip pocket where his wallet had been. Although he was grinning when he said this, I understood how he felt. The truth is, committing to having any work done is a form of investment . . . in yourself. You're worth it.

Consider three things. First, you will never know what something is going to cost until you ask. Second, whatever you do, it is going to cost money. Maybe you should consider taking out a loan to finance the project. If the project looks like it will be more than you can afford, ask the designer about scaling back on the size of the project, finding less expensive choices, or doing it in yearly increments. Time goes by so fast, and your financial state should improve with time. Third, life is filled with challenges; when you are confronted with having to stretch a bit to get something that you really want, in my experience, that is precisely when you should do it.

FEAR

What are you really afraid of? Is it fear of the unknown? Fear of not getting what you want? Not getting it right? Not being happy with the finished job? Maybe it's the fear that you will run out of money. That you will make mistakes. That you won't get along with the designer.

All of these concerns are rational, and everyone can expect to have one or more of them at some point in the progress of a project. Meeting with and talking to a professional interior designer gets these concerns out in the open so that they can be looked at and discussed frankly. Part of a designer's training is to be aware of these fears. You need to open up, speak about them, and then hear what the designer tells you to realistically expect.

Instead of fearing the unknown, find the excitement in it, the surprise of experiencing real change in your life. No one makes all the right choices all the time. *Ever*. So don't be so hard on yourself when something or someone doesn't work out as well as expected. If you have to make a painful change, realize that, in the end, you are being guided to a better decision. Things always work out for the best, even if you don't see it right away.

What's the worst that can happen if you find yourself financially strapped or simply tapped out? You will put the project on hold and wait until things improve. A designer would much rather have to deal with a temporary halt, knowing that eventually a job will reactivate, than have everything go belly up. Once a project has been started, the designer has already made a major investment in creativity and time—things that are irrecoverable costs—so the designer has extra motivation to try to help a client work out a suitable financial arrangement.

Fear is the great inhibitor to getting anything done in life. Fear creates procrastination. Procrastination traps you in a state of indecision and inaction. The only way to break free of this bondage is to start saying yes . . . and set a date for yourself. Tuesday I am calling that designer to make an appointment for an interview. Tonight I am signing the contract and sending the check. Saturday, at 1:00 p.m., I am looking at kitchen showrooms and I will get the name of a designer to call. Write it down. Do it.

Why People Call Interior Designers

Now let's look at problems that actually move people to seek professional help. These are problems found in the interior itself. I have identified seven of the most common problems found in today's interiors. They are as follows:

1 Awkward floor plan
2 Out-of-date kitchen and/or bathroom
3 Problem windows
4 Lack of space/storage
5 Inadequate electricity and electrical conveniences
6 Low light and/or poor view
7 Lack of or poor architectural details

Any one of these conditions can be significantly improved with the aid of a professional interior designer. Perhaps you have only one or two of the above problems to deal with, or maybe you have all seven. Your first thought is probably to do it yourself. Ask yourself honestly if you have the talent and training to seriously tackle these design issues. If you answer yes, you probably do. But do you have the time and patience to do it? Now you're not sure. But what you do have are ideas. Perhaps you've started a file of images that you've culled from design magazines—examples of rooms, colors, or furniture that you like. Maybe you have a folder where you keep snippets and clippings of fabrics and paint chips that appeal to you. If you are already doing any of this, you're off to a great start.

Perhaps you only have a concept about what you would like to do—but you just don't know how to begin. Consulting a professional designer can make all the difference in whether you ever get it started or ever get it done, or how good it will look when it's finished. Let's see how a designer can help you.

AWKWARD FLOOR PLAN
An awkward or poorly laid-out floor plan can mean issues with either the arrangement of the furniture or the design of the room itself. A designer is able to redefine and redesign it for you. This can be as simple as reworking your existing furniture into a new layout with an on-the-spot suggestion and some moving around. Or you might need to have the designer measure all of your furnishings, including the room itself, so that he or she can draw up a totally different floor plan.

Is the problem with the room itself or how the house is laid out? Could moving or eliminating a wall(s) open up the space? How would the traffic flow change if you relocated a door opening or perhaps covered one? Maybe your space needs new walls to create and define additional areas. What about building an addition that would go up, out, or down?

One of the most important things a designer brings to you and your space is an unbiased, open-minded outlook. It is extremely difficult to be objective about yourself, the way you live, and your possessions. But the single most important element a designer brings to a project is ideas, not criticism. All design starts with an idea.

OUT-OF-DATE KITCHEN AND/OR BATHROOM

A designer sees a space and right away starts getting ideas. Most people are unable to visualize a finished room when they see empty space. With regard to kitchens and bathrooms, a designer can size up the situation rather quickly to determine whether what you want to do is realistic or not.

Is it possible to expand the room? How can you change the traffic flow? Are you up for a complete "gut" job or will a basic face-lift do the trick? What about the financial aspect: can you afford to do this? And, ultimately, will you survive it? Kitchen and bathroom remodels are almost impossible to do yourself, especially if you are trying to use parts of those rooms while they are being remodeled. Time is of the essence with those two rooms, and a designer can move things along much faster than you would yourself.

A designer also has ideas that can help you choose surface finishes (e.g., tile, stone, glass, paint, wall covering), colors, and how best to organize the room spatially. And a designer is extremely helpful with the critical issue of whom you should hire to get the job done.

PROBLEM WINDOWS

A designer can quickly assess what the real concerns are about the windows and can make the right suggestions that will resolve light, privacy,

ABOVE LEFT: A conventional kitchen in need of an update. *Photo © 2008 by Diane Bianchini.*

BELOW LEFT: The same kitchen now looking very shipshape by way of traditional styling and contemporary details. *Design: Dream Windows & Interiors LLC.; photo © 2008 by Diane Bianchini.*

ABOVE RIGHT: Here a guest bedroom has the basic ingredients for a comfortable room. *Photo © 2008 by Judith Fox.*

BELOW RIGHT: Now we have not only comfort but savvy style and luxury in this room where guests will love to linger. *Design: Markham Interiors; photo © 2008 by Judith Fox.*

and view issues. Problems of this nature frequently require two or even three different layers of window coverings, each one meant to specifically resolve one of these issues.

Other questions about windows focus on whether to eliminate or add windows, whether to use window treatments or none at all. A frequent problem is where there are different styles and sizes of windows in the same room. An expert can bring harmony into such a space and can give you a unified design. Few things have as much impact in a room as the windows and how they are treated.

LACK OF SPACE/STORAGE

A designer can design, create, expand, or produce a better storage space than you ever possibly imagined. With information about what you have

ABOVE: What could be more clever and ingenious than this thimble-sized home office housed in a bookshelf?

Design: Inspired Style; photo ©
2008 by Ivy D. Photography, Inc.

and what you want or need, a designer can then orchestrate that into a planned design.

From rearranging an existing closet to building a walk-in closet complex, from designing shelf units to creating a home office or developing entire offices, an interior designer sees space, how to organize it, and ways to create even more space. A designer works with you to design solutions for your specific needs. Write down your list of the storage problems that you most want to improve, and then step back and let a designer work magic. Here are some examples to start your wish list:

» Custom-fit drawers for your silver
» A television hidden away, yet accessible
» A display area for your favorite collection
» Shelf space for all your books (or shoes)
» A place for your dog(s) to nap
» A place for your pet(s) to eat that can also disappear
» Filing space for everyone on your staff
» Easy access storage for unsightly stuff that you want to cover up
» Separate dressing areas for each person in your home
» A place for smelly workout clothes and shoes

INADEQUATE ELECTRICITY AND ELECTRICAL CONVENIENCES

For most of us, electricity and related electrical issues are essentially money issues. The days when you ran extension cords around the room or taped a cord across the ceiling to a hanging light fixture are gone. When you need additional outlets in a wall, ceiling, or floor, increased amperage to run all of your electrical equipment, or additional switches, you need someone to design an electrical layout. That person may be an interior designer or a lighting designer. An electrical layout is a plan on which each electrical device is located so that everything matches up with your furniture floor plan and facilitates the traffic flow. And don't forget a dimming system or, at the very least, dimmer switches.

Any electrical upgrade costs money. Light fixtures and devices (switches, outlets, etc.) cost money. The installation costs money. But this is money so well spent. You will never regret it. You will utterly love the convenience of having quiet, attractive light switches located at doorways or next to the bed, enough outlets for your kitchen appliances, an easy-to-reach spot to recharge cell phone batteries, and light levels that can be lowered or raised. You will only wish you had done it sooner.

LOW LIGHT AND/OR POOR VIEW

Light and view conditions and the direction a window faces are locked into the architecture of the building, and there isn't a lot that can be done to change either. But the conditions, no matter what they are, can be improved with a professional evaluation.

A designer is trained to look beyond what you are confronted with, to search for solutions and ideas that will make a poor view less noticeable or even disappear. Certainly, a professional can help you add lighting to counteract a dim environment. There have been times when the best solution has been to completely cover a window to gain an uninterrupted wall or block a view. Often a designer will suggest something so innovative and radical that it probably wouldn't have occurred to you.

LACK OF ARCHITECTURAL DETAIL

If you have a residence where architectural detail is missing—maybe there never was any or maybe it was all removed in a previous renovation—you can usually replace it quite easily. This is an area where a designer is critical. Your designer will give you the right components in the right style and, most importantly, in the right dimension, so that when everything is installed, it is in the right proportion for the room.

LEFT: The pair of red lampshades is an inexpensive solution that adds a generous scoop of sizzle to this living room. *Design: Claudia Dowling Interiors; photo © 2008 by Ivy D. Photography, Inc.*

ABOVE RIGHT: A clean, visually effective entrance hall. *Photo © 2008 by Matt Wargo Photography.*

BELOW RIGHT: Look what happens as paneling and several select accessories are added to turn it into a richly welcoming experience. *Design: Michelle Wenitsky Interior Design; photo © 2008 by Matt Wargo Photography.*

What a Designer Brings to the Project

Having taken a brief overview of seven of the most common problems found in interior spaces today, and of ways in which a designer can help solve those problems, let's look at some of the more intangible things a designer brings to a project.

A DESIGNER SAVES YOU MONEY

Sometimes when the price of something seems beyond your reach, you need to step back and ask yourself whether tackling it yourself will produce the results you want. How important is having the right result? Will you decide on a compromise solution that, over time, will always be a nagging reminder of a poor decision on your part? Will waiting simply mean that it will cost more later on?

Most designers can help you through a situation like this. Frequently there are alternate ways that can be explored and changes that can be made in the design to lower the cost. Sometimes you just need to see the project in perspective.

A few years ago a client of mine wanted to turn his dining room into a library. He wanted everything paneled in wood with a wood finish and as many shelves as possible. I came up with a design to maximize the space, and I priced it out with a custom cabinetmaker. The price was high . . . the room had a few challenging problems. Plus, it was all wood-finished cabinetry, not painted, and a fairly involved design. Needless to say, he was floored with the price and decided not to go ahead with it.

Sometime later, with my permission, he took the design to a local retail cabinet shop to see what they could do for him. He wound up with two separate bookcase units made by this shop.

Later I saw what he had done. The two bookcase units were facing each other: one in an English-style walnut finish, and the other painted white with French ornamental details. I asked him if he was happy with the way the two cabinets looked in the room. He said no. He had already exceeded the shelf space and needed more bookshelves! I asked him if he wanted to reconsider the original idea. It would mean losing the two shelf units and starting over. He said yes to it all.

So, now we were back where we started, only he had spent a great deal of money on two bookshelf units that were discarded, the price to construct the room design had increased, and he had missed the enjoyment of living in a wood-paneled library for three or four years.

In the long run he would have saved time as well as money. The illustration could just as easily have been about a window treatment, a fabric or piece of furniture, an addition to the house, or a totally new kitchen or bath.

Remember, a designer is in a position to do the following:

» Be objective about what you want
» Give you a professional assessment of your situation
» Help you develop a solid plan of action.

A DESIGNER CULTIVATES AND DEVELOPS YOUR PERSONAL LIFESTYLE

I don't think very many people have a good sense of where they are when it comes to style. Style is what a designer is all about. A designer's perception of your information will give you a changed environment.

How is style defined? First of all, style is a reflection of your personal beliefs. It is a gathering of what has been in your life, of what you would like to have in relation to where you are right now. Style makes the case for the choices you are making about how you want others to see you.

Style is a reflection of your attitudes that, in turn, are reflected in how you live. How you dress is another giveaway. Yet style is something you can arbitrarily select. You can change it if you don't like it—you can reinvent yourself. You can redefine yourself next month if you wish.

Working with a designer, your style evolves and becomes defined as you go through the selection process. As you talk to your designer about what appeals to you, a designer hears and sees things about you that you can't. By making suggestions,

. . . style is a reflection of your personal beliefs. It is a gathering of what has been in your life, of what you would like to have in relation to where you are right now.

Style Categories	
YOU ARE	**YOU WANT TO COME HOME TO**
Self-reliant, successful	A sleek, professionally finished space in a refined, elegant color scheme
Socially adept, gregarious	An eclectic, colorful, comfortable, inviting interior; warm colors
Organized	Everything in its place, lots of built-ins; every closet fully finished; smooth surfaces; natural colors
Fashionable, a Mr. and/or Mrs. First-nighter	A stylish, exotic interior with lots of sparkle and dramatic lighting
Serene, spiritually centered	A calm, soothing environment, with cool, quiet colors
Easy going, unchallenged	A nice place, but not fussy or really "done"; comfort is everything; color is good

asking questions, showing different types of furnishings and images, and monitoring responses, your designer puts it all together and is able to help define your style.

Your style starts to be shaped, formulated, and cultivated until it becomes tangible—something you can feel. It becomes the place you want to come home to, because it really is you. And it makes you feel good. That's what design is supposed to do. In the accompanying sidebar is a chart of style categories that will help you identify your style and what design direction you might take.

A DESIGNER GUIDES YOU IN
THE ACQUISITION OF FINE ART

Many designers are specialists in the purchase of artwork and antiques. Some are wonderfully knowledgeable about period styles and historical information. Others specialize in selecting modern art and artifacts. Their advice can be very helpful in guiding you when you wish to buy

artwork. This type of purchase is considered a financial investment and should be approached as such. Unless you are already a specialist in a particular genre and an expert buyer, you would be well advised to work with an experienced professional designer who has this expertise.

It's not enough to fall in love with a piece or to want to buy something because it's at a great price. It has to work in your space. A painting has to be an appropriate size to go over the sofa. A table must be the right size and shape for the area. A chandelier should neither be too big nor too small for where it's going to hang.

Consult with a designer at the very beginning of your project so that you both can map out a plan for making purchases. You want to make sure that what you purchase is something that you really like, something that has investment potential, and something that is going to enhance your interior decor.

In addition to having the expertise to guide you in this type of purchase, a designer usually

also has long-term relationships with specific dealers, shops, and vendors, often on a global basis. The designer lets the vendor know when he is looking for a specific item, and the dealer lets the designer know when a shipment is coming in or when a requested item has been located. The value of this kind of networking is something you cannot acquire by going online.

A DESIGNER HELPS YOU WORK WITH AN ARCHITECT, HOMEBUILDER, OR CONTRACTOR

Why do you need an interior designer if you are planning to work with an architect, a homebuilder, or a contractor? After all, they each deal with space. An architect designs an exterior shell and divides the interior into appropriated spaces. A homebuilder builds from the architect's plans. A contractor constructs the interior shell according to plans designed by others.

But do they understand space from the standpoint of a human being living in it? An interior designer instinctively understands spatial relationships and can tell when something about a space is not going to work. A designer understands how space is meant to flow from room to room, the inherent relationship between rooms, the way you move through a room, and, ultimately, how a room will look with furniture in it.

It is vital that you bring in a professional designer to review your proposed floor plans *before* the drawings reach the "final approval" stage. This way, at the very least, a designer can "eyeball" your plans and drawings just to make sure that everything is working the way you envision it. If it's not, you will still have time to make changes.

Ideally, your designer should be brought in at the *beginning* of the space planning-and-development stage. That way, your designer works with your architect, homebuilder, and/or contractor, and together they design a strong, cohesive floor plan. In this ideal scenario, each one comes to the table with special areas of expertise, and everyone benefits from this collection of talent—especially you. Together they are able to consolidate ideas and decide the most economical way to design your project.

A DESIGNER CAN BE PIVOTAL IN SELLING YOUR RESIDENCE

When you plan to put a house or an apartment on the market, plan first to get a professional assessment of the interior. You need to make your home look its absolute best. As Will Rogers once said, "You never get a second chance at a first impression." With professional guidance you will be able to have your home looking its best without spending a lot of money. It is commonly accepted today that the best chance of selling your property for the highest price comes in the first three to four weeks it's on the market, when there's the most activity. *Do not wait until the property is on the market to seek professional help.* The length of time it takes to sell a property, and the price it ultimately sells for, is what makes the venture profitable or not.

The key, again, is objectivity. An interior designer can see right away what areas need to be improved. A designer is objective about the space and is not emotionally attached to a certain wall color or Aunt Mabel's Victorian table. If it's not working for the space, it's working *against* you and the sale. The designer sees what it would take to make the space appealing and can assess the most expedient and economical ways to get it done. And if that means changing the color of the walls or stowing Aunt Mabel's table temporarily, then you need to trust your designer's expertise in the matter.

This type of interior designing is generally referred to as home staging or house dressing.

These are but five more ways in which a designer can help you, and reason enough to get over the hurdles of inertia, resistance, procrastination, and fear.

A number of years ago an acquaintance bought a lamp that needed a lampshade. As most people would, she went out and bought one. Easy. The minute she got it home she knew it was wrong. So she called a friend who is an interior designer and asked for help. Her friend came over, took one look at it, unplugged the lamp, and off they went with the lamp to have a shade made.

The finished custom-made shade was beautiful, and this woman was amazed at how much she learned from this one single experience. It never occurred to her that in order to have a shade sized correctly for a lamp, you must take the lamp to the lampshade place. She couldn't believe how difficult it was to properly size a lampshade, even with the lamp in front of her. She was awed by how much a designer has to know, even on what appears to be the simplest matters. She also discovered that she had much more confidence in deciding what she liked in the way of furnishings, because the designer gave her a level of comfort that she had not known before. She knew that things would look right—as they always do—with professional guidance, and, lastly, she knew she could rely on that.

It is vital that you bring in a professional designer to review your proposed floor plans *before* the drawings reach the "final approval" stage.

Two

In the Beginning there was Reality. Now there is reality TV. Interior designing being done for TV gives a false impression of the entire process. The time frame in which everything appears to magically come together is forced. This is not how it is in the very real world of interior design.

In the real world there are often harsh realities to be faced. On a project, with workmen as part of the picture, one discovers quickly that they, in fact, turn out to be human. They get colds, they are often messy, and they don't show up when they're supposed to. Things are installed wrong, and they have to be corrected or redone. This takes time . . . and money. Another harsh reality is that everything costs more than you thought, takes longer, and is far more problematic to accomplish than you ever expected. Why is it that so many things go wrong so often? A friend explained that if you could really see everyone who is involved in producing just one item, you would be looking at a cast of hundreds. For example, it's Monday morning, and a lumberjack suffering from a hangover should have stayed home. Instead he is out in the forest. Judgment impaired, he marks a tree to be cut that should be left standing. This tree is cut down and now goes through all the processes that ultimately bring it to a lumber mill, where it is marked for a furniture manufacturer. Many more people are now involved as the wood is milled, fashioned, finished, and selected to be used in a table. Now the woodworkers cut, shape, and craft it into a table, where our piece of wood becomes a leg for a table. More people are involved in the finishing of the table: the sanding, staining, and spraying of the finishes. Now the table is prepared for shipping, which involves more people inspecting, wrapping, packing, and crating before it is loaded onto a truck and heads for your city. Its next stop is a warehouse, where it is unwrapped, inspected, rewrapped, and prepared for local delivery to your residence. At last, it is unloaded from a truck and carried into your home, where it is once more unwrapped, this time for you to look at it. You agree it's beautiful and was worth the wait. Within forty-eight hours, a split in the wood of one table leg appears.

Why? The tree should not have been cut; it was too green, too young. It did not cure well; and when it entered your environment and encountered a traumatizing climate change, it finally split open, revealing the inherent problem. The point is, at any step along the way, the odds of any one thing going wrong are amazingly high. It is a miracle that anything is delivered trouble-free.

I've often joked about what the silkworms on the mulberry trees have for lunch, because lunch eventually becomes the silk taffeta for the curtains

FACING: A double-height eating area at one end of a kitchen has built-in drama without being pretentious.
Design: Room Services Designs, Inc.; photo © 2008 by Phillip Ennis Photography.

that I plan to use in a living room. On reality TV, deliveries happen on time. In reality design, most things are delayed. But the good news is that they do arrive. If you base your expectations on what you see on TV design shows, you will always be frustrated and displeased. Look at interior design as a process that takes time, that needs you in order to be complete, and where the process itself provides its own sense of fulfillment.

Define the Project

Before you actually engage an interior designer, you need a clear idea of what you want to accomplish. When you and the designer meet, you will then be able to discuss your specific goals and ideas. The designer needs as much relevant information as possible about your project in order to develop a proposal for working with you.

The initial meetings with the designer serve to create a list of everything that you want to have done. This information then turns into a document called a **scope of work.** It needs to be very accurate, as all future estimates and bids will be based

in terms of broad brushstrokes: I need to have the dining room painted and wall covering put up; or, it's time to renovate the bathroom. Decide what rooms or areas are going to be worked on and then focus on the basic work you want to have done. The details will get worked out as you move through the design process.

Let's use a bathroom renovation as an example. You have already made the major decisions for the ceiling, walls, and floor finishes. What's next? You and the designer decide if you should replace major pieces in the room: the tub, the sink, and the toilet. Next, you move to the fittings, Do you want a wall-mounted or counter faucet for the sink? A deck- or wall-mounted tub spout? What finish do you want them in? Chrome or nickel, brushed or polished, brass or gold? What about the style of the handle? Should it be a lever, a faceted ball, or a spoke-style handle? How about the type and style of the spout? What accessories do you want: towel bars, tissue holders, robe hooks?

The above sequence gives you an idea of the thought process that you and the designer will go through in developing the design. As you can see, there are many parts and pieces that make up the design process. Always keep in mind the

---

Once you have a clear idea of the work you want done, think about how life will be once the work starts.

---

on the items in your scope of work. It is the method by which your project is kept on track. Your scope of work becomes the bible for your project.

It is hard to capture every single thing that needs to be done. You will find yourself thinking of things in the middle of the night, while you're driving, or when you're in the shower. Write them down as soon as you can. It is okay to keep adding things to the list even as the project progresses. You need to get on paper just as many things as possible. It is the only way you and the designer will stay on top of the job. But you aren't responsible for remembering everything; that is why you are hiring a professional. Part of the designer's job is to help you create and continually develop the scope of work and not forget anything.

How do you get a clear idea of what you want to accomplish? First, focus on the big picture. Think

major vision of what you are planning to do. As you and the designer spend time together, talk about your project, and make decisions together, you will see that, item by item, everything falls into place.

Prepare to Do It

Once you have a clear idea of the work you want done, think about how life will be once the work starts. Will the excitement of finally having the work done carry you through a period of stressful inconvenience? Or will the inconvenience really be inconvenient? Do you know your tolerance level for having your home in disarray for an extended period?

ABOVE: Once a screened-in porch, this is now a year-round family room. *Design: Roeder Design Group; photo © 2008 by Don Pearse Photographers, Inc.*

FACING: The only ingredient missing in this inviting entertainment room is the popcorn. *Design: Michelle Wenitsky Interior Design; photo © 2008 by Matt Wargo Photography.*

This is very important. When everything seems to be turned upside down in your home and covered with dust, people often experience a feeling of loss of control. For some people, just knowing that the current situation is not going to be forever gets them through a tough period. For others, having dust everywhere on everything is a demoralizing experience, and they don't handle it well.

Do not underestimate the power of dust. Keep sponges and a broom handy. At the end of the day, sweep up and know that tomorrow will be the same. But it's not forever. Morale is important. Even if everything is covered over with paper, plastic, drop cloths, and/or Masonite boards, if it's dusted and swept each day and the everyday debris of beverage bottles, containers, packing materials, and newspapers is picked up and disposed of, it becomes bearable.

If your budget allows, hire someone to come in and do the cleaning. Or hire a contractor and work people who maintain neat, clean job sites. Yes, they do exist. It is such a pleasure to see a job site swept and picked up at the end of the day— it's the sign of those who take pride in their work and really care about the work team and you.

How will the project impact the rest of your home? Will you need to close off a room or two or even an entire section for a while? What if "for a while" turns into an extended period? Do you have a contingency plan that will help you cope should this happen? Should areas adjacent to the work area be protected or put off-limits? Will you be able to successfully protect and/or store pieces of furniture, other furnishings, and accessories that are currently in the work area? You may need to budget in the rental of a storage unit.

If your project is a full-scale renovation and involves the entire house or apartment, are you planning to live in it while the work is being done? Should you make other living arrangements? Think about being without a kitchen, bedroom, or bathroom—how will that impact your eating, sleeping, and bathing requirements? Do you have another place to sleep? Do you have an alternate water source? Access to a toilet or a shower? Can you set up a temporary mini-kitchen in the living room or the laundry room? Some people have solved these problems with the help of neighbors, friends, health or country clubs, or by renting a trailer to park in the driveway—literally, a home away from home. If your plans are extensive enough to require your vacating the premises for a while, factor the additional costs of your living elsewhere and eating out into your decorating budget.

If your renovation work will require a shut down of water or electricity for a day or two, contractors can usually arrange to leave you with temporary hookups (water and electrical) overnight. The areas that disrupt a household the most are kitchens, bathrooms, and floors. If your renovation includes these areas, plan carefully, as unforeseen events and site conditions can arise and upset the best-laid plans.

Should you consider including other areas that need work? Would this be a good time to think about upgrading the windows or the HVAC (heating/ventilation/air conditioning) system, for example? If you're recovering the living room furniture, are there other rooms where pieces are in need of repair as well? Are you wallpapering and/or painting? Should you include closets and adjacent areas, like a hall or foyer, along with the main area? Including as many things as you can afford into the scope of work will maximize the work effort and save you time and money in the long run. You will also have a longer period of enjoyment/relief before things need to be repaired or replaced again.

Consider Other Design Professionals

From the moment you start thinking about having work done, realize you might require additional professional services to fix or advise on architectural, structural, audio/visual, lighting, or plumbing problems. Will your kitchen renovation require taking down a wall or two or perhaps the reverse, building a wall to create a wine cellar or pantry where none exists now? Would you like to put in a powder room? Do you dream of pushing out a wall to extend a room? How about combining two apartments into one by buying the

apartment next door or upstairs? Maybe you're thinking about adding a room or wing over an existing part of the house? Any of these scenarios will require the services of an interior designer, an architect, and, most likely, a structural engineer.

Let's assume that you and an interior designer have created a plan that includes major renovation work. An architect should review the plan to make sure that it can be implemented. An architect has to file plans when walls are demolished, moved, or built; when plumbing is moved or added; when ceiling or floors are altered to add a staircase or elevator; or if electrical renovations, fireplaces, or additions to the house are planned. If you have designed the plans yourself, they will still need to be filed and checked by a building inspector to make sure they follow local codes.

No matter where you live today, you will be required to file your plans. The architect files plumbing, electrical, and lighting plans; demolition drawings; door, window, and hardware schedules; and all construction drawings, including cabinetry. Ideally, an architect and an interior designer collaborate on a plan together. That way, when the interior designer creates the interior, the architect can make it happen from a structural standpoint or vice versa. They work out problem areas together, refine the plans, and produce a tightly constructed set of plans that won't need changes or redrawing later on.

If you are renovating any room, even the bathroom, you will probably be in need of an audiovisual consultant. Since audiovisual and computer technologies change so rapidly, the advice of a professional will be invaluable. Whether you are planning to create a home theater or just update your home office, a professional audiovisual consultant can help with selecting the components, wiring the system, and installing it all. If you rely on the guy who sells you the TV or computer, and advice from a neighbor or a relative, you are fostering a "make-do" attitude. Making do is rarely satisfactory except on a short-term basis. Realize it's time to hire a professional and have it done right.

People often hesitate hiring an outside consultant because of the cost. They are reluctant to spend money on something they perceive to be intangible. Initially, yes, there is something intangible about working with a consultant. Here you are, paying by the hour for someone to poke around the house to figure out the best way to do something. Truth is, there are times when you have to bite the bullet, pay the price, and trust someone. What you are actually paying for is that person's expertise and experience, intangible on one level but something that will produce the right results. Your designer is your advisor and can be very helpful in explaining when you need to bring in an outside consultant.

Electrical and lighting alterations are long lasting and cannot be easily changed. Plan carefully . . . and early. Electrical work especially has to be done early in the project because other work cannot proceed until the walls and ceilings are closed up and ready for finishing. Wiring requires opening the walls and ceilings or, if you have new construction, leaving the walls and ceilings open until all wiring is finished. Once the wiring is completed and the walls and ceilings are closed, any changes that you make to the locations of outlets or switches becomes a costly addition.

Whether you need a lighting designer or not depends on the size of the project and the level of expertise your interior designer has when it comes to lighting. On small projects, the designer and a good electrician may be all that are needed. For large-scale projects, the architect's office, usually working in conjunction with a lighting designer and an interior designer, will produce reflected ceiling plans and electrical layouts. Frequently, the designer's firm will engage a lighting designer to develop a lighting plan to work with your furniture floor plan. When the two plans are integrated, you have a carefully thought-out, custom-designed plan for your interior. This way, you are far less likely to have to change things later on. Home security systems, dimming systems, and kitchen and bath wiring are all part of today's interiors and need to be professionally designed. Your best route is to always ask your designer.

Structural engineers are called in when there are issues involving load-bearing walls, building or shoring up retaining walls, adding weight to

Your designer is your advisor and can be very helpful in explaining when you need to bring in an outside consultant.

an existing floor, or figuring the snow load a roof or deck can bear. Pouring concrete, excavating a basement, creating a patio, installing a whirlpool bathtub, adding large plants to a terrace or balcony, or moving in a grand piano are all items that usually require the approval of a structural engineer. In many cases, a town or city's building requirements will need the stamp of a structural engineer on your plans before they can be filed for approval. Seek direction from your architect or designer.

Once you understand that your project is going to need one or more of these professionals, ask for referrals. More than likely your designer will already know and have worked with an architect, an audiovisual consultant, a lighting designer, a kitchen/bath designer, and a structural engineer, or can make inquiries about finding one. Take advantage of professionals who have established working relationships.

The Design File

One of the most important tools you will need is a design and decorating file. This is an actual file folder or envelope that you create for yourself and your project. Put in pictures of things you like and don't like. This helps clarify your thinking and gives very insightful information to the designer. Include swatches of fabrics, paint colors, and anything that appeals to you: pictures of

Take an Inventory

Every homeowner should have a picture inventory of his or her possessions along with relevant serial numbers. The most obvious reason is for insurance purposes. In the event that there is a dispute about an item, producing a picture of it can be a lifesaver. If you file a claim for damage or loss, concrete proof of ownership is imperative. All too frequently, there is a need to prove the authenticity of what you say and what may or may not have happened to the item. If something gets broken or is damaged, you will be able to prove what it looked like "before," which can be especially helpful when having the piece repaired or reupholstered.

A second reason to take an inventory is the added value that you will bring to the designer. Every project, large or small, requires a catalog of the client's furniture that will be reused in the new project. If you have photographs and measurements of your furnishings, you will be that much more ahead (and so will your designer). It becomes very easy to flip through the pictures or review them on a CD to determine what could be

> ## Once you understand that your project is going to need one or more of these professionals, ask for referrals.

houses, of rooms and interior spaces, of gardens and landscaping, of individual pieces of furniture, of current, vintage, or antique items, and of furnishings of every description.

If your project includes many rooms, have a folder for each room. This is where you will also keep your lists, reminders and notes, your scope of work. I use transparent string envelopes (found in any office supply store) with my own clients, and I have one for every room that we are working on.

Some clients use an accordion-type file for organizing proposals and invoices. You can file either by month, by invoice or proposal number, or by room. Building or renovation creates a lot of paperwork, and you need some method of recordkeeping.

good to use versus what should be discarded or moved to another part of the house.

The third reason to do an inventory is the ease with which you will be able to access the information about a particular item. Begin a lifelong habit of cataloging your possessions. You may already have lists, and possibly pictures, of major items for insurance policies. However, the inventory I'm referring to is a working document consisting of groups and categories, a documentation of everything you own. Let's get started.

PHOTOGRAPHING YOUR POSSESSIONS
Don't use a video camera for this project, as you will want still photographs that you can study and make prints of. If you use a digital camera, you can keep your photos organized on disks.

I mark one disk for pictures of rooms and furniture. Another disk has pictures of accessories and personal items.

Try to keep things in order; shoot one room and its furnishings completely before you move on to the next. First, take overall shots of the room or area. Start in a corner and shoot the opposite wall. Move to the next corner and shoot the opposite wall. Keep moving around the room until you have recorded the entire space. If your camera doesn't have a wide-angle lens, you may need to take pictures that overlap one another until you have covered one entire wall. Try to stay the same distance away from the wall for each shot. It is easier to view the running sequence of a wall when the ceiling and floor run in approximately the same line from shot to shot.

Shooting the overall pictures first focuses your vision on the contents of the room. Next, you will photograph the furniture, moving around the room in an orderly way. Before you start this process, you will find it helpful to create a furniture list. This way you won't overlook an item.

For valuable pieces, take several pictures from different angles and a close-up of special details. If you are thinking of selling an item in the future, be sure to document it with a lot of pictures. Whether you're going to use eBay, an antique shop, or an auction house, the more detail you are able to provide the vendor or buyer, the more easily you can sell the piece.

MEASURING YOUR FURNITURE

Once you have finished shooting everything in the room, you will need to measure each item. Again, completely finish one room before moving on to the next.

Take a tape measure and measure each piece of furniture, putting the measurement in the appropriate column. Include mirrors, boxes, artwork, and accessories. The rule is to always measure the largest point-to-point measurement in a given direction. For the width, measure the widest point of a chest, table, or bookcase and include any moulding on the edge. For upholstered pieces such as sofas and chairs, measure from outside arm to outside arm. Measuring the height is pretty straightforward: just measure from the floor to the highest point on the back or top of the piece, including the moulding. For the depth, the measurement is taken from front to back.

Chairs and sofas are a little more tricky. With a furniture floor plan, even a half inch can determine whether a piece will work or not. Accurately measure the depth of a chair or sofa from the point that sticks out the most in the front, to the point that is sticking out the farthest in back (usually at the center).

The best way for an accurate measurement is to place the chair or sofa touching the wall. Run the tape measure under the item until it touches the wall. Measure where the widest point of the piece is, usually in front at the center, and that is the depth of the piece. If you find the tape measure is touching the baseboard instead of the wall, you will have to add the depth of the baseboard into your measurement (3/4 inch to one inch is standard).

If it is impossible to move a piece against a wall, take a tape measure or a yardstick and plumb it straight down from the uppermost part of the back of the chair or sofa to the floor. Next, run a second tape under the deepest part of the piece from the front to the yardstick or tape in the back. The more accurately you do this, the more successful will be the floor plan.

You may also find it helpful to group your furnishings by category. I keep 4 x 6-inch prints in an album format, storing them in one of two ways: organizing them according to rooms or by putting them into the following groups:

» Seating (chair, sofa, ottoman, bench, stool)
» Tables (cocktail, lamp, end, side, dining, night, writing)
» Case pieces (dresser, sideboard, armoire, secretary, desk, trunk)
» Accessories (light fixtures, books, artwork, vases, containers, bric-a-brac, mementos, and souvenirs)
» Window treatments and coverings

FACING: An intriguing mix of textures demonstrates the effectiveness of an interior designer's eye when selecting accessories. *Design: Sheridan Interiors, Inc.; photo © 2008 by Irving Solero.*

The Wish List

This is the true fun part of any project—no matter how large or small it might be. This is your chance, first of all, to really think about things you would like to have, to put a name to things that you had only briefly entertained. Second, it's your chance to get on paper all of the things you have dreamed about, even if you weren't sure they would fit or if you could afford them. Maybe you'll find that what you really need to do is move! This is your opportunity to find out.

Spend some serious time daydreaming. Let your mind wander. Drawer-type refrigerators . . . a freezer . . . two dishwashers or ovens . . . a cabinet for special appliances you might not even own yet, like an ice cream/gelato maker or an all-in-one coffee/espresso/cappuccino station. Maybe you want an icemaker machine, a wine cooler, or, better yet, a full-fledged wine pantry or cellar. Look through the magazines for the latest in equipment and appliances for the kitchen

FACING: Here, the designer uses eclectic, dynamic accessories in a forceful way to display the many interests of the owner. *Design: Richard Schlesinger Interior Designs, Inc.; photo © 2008 by Ivy D. Photography, Inc.*

LEFT: An elegant, sleek window treatment is used for the focal point of this living room. *Design: Sheridan Interiors, Inc.; photo © 2008 by David Regen.*

Furnishings Inventory—Sample List

ITEM	DESCRIPTION	WIDTH	DEPTH	HEIGHT
Sofa	Beige linen	87"	39"	32" back; 24" arm
Side chair	Victorian, cane seat	18 1/2"	20"	18" seat
Coffee table	Maple with glass top	42"	18 1/2"	17 1/2"
Dining Chairs (4)	Wood frame, upholstered seat	22"	19"	35" back; 18" seat
Bed	Pinecone finial	63 3/4"	81"	40" headboard 24" mattress
Table lamp	Alabaster vase	–	–	24" shade rest
Mirrors (2)	Bamboo frame	36"	–	39"
Chair	Spindleback	22"	23"	17" seat

or bathroom. Tear out pictures and pop them into your file.

Perhaps you've always thought about screening the porch, making a small apartment over the garage, or creating a space for an exercise area. Maybe what you wish for is a fully finished basement, complete with a mini-kitchen and powder room. On a more intimate level, maybe you would just love to have gold-plated hardware and faucets, a heated floor, marble counters, or a sauna in the bathroom. Maybe you want a mini-beverage center or ceiling speakers or a flat-screen TV in your bedroom. The point is, think about it, put the items on a list, turn the list over to your designer, and see how much you can get. Sometimes things don't cost as much as you think. And a designer can be surprisingly adept at working a lot of these items into the space. You probably won't be able to accommodate every single item on the list, but this way you have the freedom to select the things that mean the most to you.

Put a copy of your wish list into your file and the appropriate room folder. Keep the master copy with you so that you can jot down thoughts as they occur and add them to the list.

Pause for a moment. Don't you feel great? You now have a clear idea of what you want to do and a pretty good idea of how you are going to go about it. You have a folder full of images, your furnishings are inventoried, and, yes, you have ideas . . . lots of ideas. Now you know you need an interior designer and maybe other professional consultants as part of your team. You are ready to go find them.

Planning Checklist

1 Think about your wish list. Write your ideas down.

2 Create a design file. Start clipping and saving images, pictures.

3 Decide which areas or rooms require work. Write them down.

4 List the work you plan to do in each room. For example:
  » Accessorizing
  » Audio/visual equipment
  » Ceiling (painting, papering or specialty finish)
  » Closet interiors

  » Electrical work
  » Floor covering (new surface, refinish or replace existing)
  » Furniture arrangement
  » HVAC upgrade
  » Lighting
  » Plumbing
  » Rehang artwork
  » Repairs (General, minor, or furniture)
  » Replace worn-out, broken items
  » Upholstery work
  » Walls (painting, papering, or specialty finish)
  » Window treatments

5 Take a furnishings inventory: measure and record all items.

6 Take photographs of your furnishings. Catalog them.

7 Review all the above items with your interior designer.

8 When ready to begin, prepare for the work:
  » What needs to be moved, put away, or stored?
  » What needs to be protected?
  » Do provisions need to be made for sleeping, bathing, cooking?
  » Do arrangements need to be made for children and animals?
  » Confirm needed security arrangements.

Three

Architects, interior designers, and decorators all have distinct talents that they offer to help you finish or furnish your home. Sometimes the different abilities that these individuals bring to a building or remodeling project may seem a bit unclear. Your specific project requirements will let you know which ones you need to engage to get the job done.

One of the areas that always seems a bit hazy is the role that an architect, interior designer, or decorator actually has in a project. To make sure that you are clear on what you are looking for, let me define what architects, decorators, and interior designers do. Once you understand the differences, you will be in a better position to determine what you need.

Architects

Architects design buildings. Although they are primarily concerned with the exterior and structural elements of a building, they are often skilled at designing the interior built environment, especially the design of interior architectural details. Any work that involves the structure of the building or the interior structure of an apartment needs approved drawings from an architect. An architectural firm frequently will have an interior designer on staff, or a full-fledged interior design department. Architects have to be registered in the state in which they practice in order to work and file approved drawings.

Decorators

Many centuries ago, when decorating interiors became a series of defined activities, the art of interior decorating was born. Everyone who worked on the interior space was involved in creating the ornamentation for the ceiling, walls, and floors. Overall direction came from the architect, who usually had a team of skilled plasterers, gilders, painters, woodworkers, carvers, cabinetmakers, and stonemasons. As time went on, the treatment of interior spaces became known as "decoration" or "decor," and the people who did the work were called "decorators." To this day, painters, plasterers, and other

FACING: A green pear accent is the perfect touch to add a little zest to the spare, clean lines of this renovated bathroom. *Design: Atkinson + Design, Inc.; photo © 2008 by Patrick Kennedy Photography.*

tradespeople are known as decorators, and, by extension, people who work on upholstery and do window treatments are also referred to as decorators. As a profession they create the aesthetics of an interior space, the style and selection of fabrics and furnishings, as well as the colors. They do not need a license to perform these activities.

Interior Designers

For many centuries the design of the interior space, as we understand the term today, was the responsibility of the wife or the person who headed the household. Toward the latter part of the nineteenth century, a few courageous souls realized that how the interior of the home looked could involve more than paint colors, fabrics, and window treatments.

In the first quarter of the twentieth century, a handful of women actually started their own decorating and design businesses. Their vision extended from the embellishing of the ceiling down to trimming a lampshade and embracing the use of color in fresh, dynamic schemes. Today, interior design is recognized as a profession, and interior designers must be licensed or registered to practice in about half of the states in the United States.

Interior designers have to undergo rigorous training in order to pass a national qualifying design exam and must have specified educational levels and work experience in order to take it. Interior designers are trained to manage projects, and they must abide by strict professional codes of standards and conduct. Within their realm, they are responsible for protecting the health, welfare, and safety of the public. They specialize in designing a complete built interior. Their skills may include specialization in one or more of the following areas:

» Space planning
» National, state, and local building codes
» Needs of special-interest groups, such as senior citizens, children, or the disabled
» Lighting

> Interior designers have to undergo rigorous training in order to pass a national qualifying design exam and must have specified educational levels and work experience in order to take it.

» Acoustics and sound transmission
» Ergonomics
» Fire-related issues

Interior design companies will often have a staff architect as part of their design team. Many firms are headed by an interior designer who has an architect as a partner—a great combination.

How Interior Designers Work with Architects

When your project requires both an architect and an interior designer, look for a designer who has an established working relationship with an architect. Architects and designers who have worked together before know what to expect from each

RIGHT: This combined living room/dining area in an extraordinary architectural gem is built in a style called "Gothik" (because it's not really Gothic). *Design: The Baltimore Design Center; photo © 2008 by Ivy D. Photography, Inc.*

FACING: Another view of this room, where very clever accessorizing takes this space into the realm of the "WOW"! *Design: The Baltimore Design Center; photo © 2008 by Ivy D. Photography, Inc.*

other, what to look out for, and how to get the best from their respective talents.

When architects and designers collaborate at the start of a project, the interiors are designed from two points of view. Although balance, scale, and proportion in the interior space are paramount issues for both, the architect focuses on the organization of space and the interior designer on the management of space. Since they look at the same space with a different vision, the final design is one of true balance and harmony, because it incorporates both points of view.

Architects and interior designers working together becomes a system of checks and balances. An interior designer is given a set of the architect's plans. The designer reviews the plans to make sure that the interior elements such as door openings, windows, and wall dimensions are balanced; that there is flow of movement through the space; that the proposed plan accommodates the furniture as drawn in the floor plan; and that all electrical and lighting needs have been addressed.

Interior designers verify architectural elements. Is the architectural detailing or spacing around windows designed so that a window treatment can be installed, for example? Dimensions are thoroughly checked and details are worked out with the designer and the architect so that the revised drawings accurately reflect the requirements. Sometimes there are site conditions, even with new construction, that can restrict the proposed plans.

In the case of renovating an existing space, hidden structural elements need to be discovered early on so that your proposed floor plan can be executed. Here the collaboration of an electrician, a plumber, and possibly an engineer, together with the architect and the designer, may be needed to deal with intrusive structural elements such as supporting walls, heating conduits, water pipes, and electrical wiring.

The benefit of this arrangement is that by having both an architect and interior designer, you have talented, creative minds meshing skills and visions together, a combination that produces an integrated, beautifully built environment. The beneficiary is you.

WAYS AN INTERIOR DESIGNER CAN HELP YOU

The following is a list of areas where the engagement of an interior design office will be of great benefit:

- » Accessorizing
- » Artwork purchases
- » Bathroom design and renovation
- » Bed treatments
- » Cabinetry and built-ins
- » Cleaning/ maintenance/ repair instructions
- » Closet interiors
- » Color schemes and finishes
- » Custom furniture
- » Customized bedding and linens
- » Drafting/drawing/ elevations/ measuring
- » Electrical work/ improvements/ upgrades
- » Entertainment/ recreation rooms
- » Fabric schemes
- » Floor plans
- » Floor refinishing
- » Furniture layouts
- » Furniture refinishing, polishing, repairing, or replating
- » Historical renovation/ restoration
- » Home office
- » Home staging
- » Home theatre
- » Kitchen design and renovation
- » Lampshades
- » Lighting plans
- » Mouldings and ornamental detail
- » Office space planning and design
- » Painting and wallpapering
- » Problem solving
- » Refurbishment of existing furnishings
- » Renovation work
- » Restoration of floors, paneling, furniture, plasterwork, or antiques
- » Room arrangements
- » Space planning
- » Upholstery work
- » Wall arrangements: framing, hanging, and placement of artwork
- » Wall treatments (special finishes, wall coverings, wall upholstery)
- » Window treatments

Naturally, interior designer services are essential for all businesses (whether hospitality, medical,

Architects and interior designers working together becomes a system of checks and balances.

FACING: The intriguing locations for the windows really brings the country into this country-style kitchen. They also provide a continually changing backdrop. *Design: Michelle Wenitsky Interior Design; photo © 2008 by Matt Wargo Photography.*

retail, hotel, senior housing, shopping centers, or restaurants) to make the business area as appealing and functional as possible.

WHEN TO CONTACT AN ARCHITECT

You need to contact an architect if you plan to do any of the following:

- » Alter structural elements
- » Build a house or an addition
- » Build an interior elevator, staircase, or fireplace
- » Demolish a house or the interior of an apartment or house
- » Design interior architectural detail and ornament
- » File a bathroom, kitchen, lighting,
- or plumbing renovation plan
- » Install security and communications systems
- » Move walls, windows, doors, or plumbing
- » Plan extensive renovations
- » Restore or preserve a building, roofing, or exterior ornament

Get referrals of other clients the designer has worked with. Naturally, your final evaluation of a designer should always be an interview.

WHEN TO HIRE A DECORATOR

If your plans are more basic, contact a decorating company or shop. But, no matter how elementary the work you are planning, it is wisest to first consult a professional interior designer. Hire one for a single hour and see how much clearer your thinking will be. In addition to helping you focus, the designer will give you suggestions and ideas that will take what you envision and enhance it. Decorating companies are helpful in the following areas:

- » Bed treatments
- » Painting
- » Upholstery work
- » Wallpapering
- » Window treatments

The Search

REFERRALS

The best and easiest way to find an interior designer is to ask people you know for a referral. However, you must evaluate the opinion of those making the recommendations. Are they people you trust? Do you value their opinion? Do you think the same way about things or at least have a similar set of values? What is their sense of quality, where is their barometer set for taste level? Are they on a similar financial scale as you? If the answers to these questions indicate a positive commonality, you are probably wise to pursue the referral. However, a designer is trained to work with all types of people with all levels of income, so don't negate a referral just because the referring person has a different personality from yours.

You might need to investigate further if someone you know speaks demeaningly about a designer and a project. Is the problem really the designer, or could it possibly be the client? Ask yourself truthfully if the referring person might be impatient, difficult to work with, demanding, or even a trifle obnoxious? One way to assess the referral, without having to get into gory details, is to get the designer's name and telephone number and call. Get referrals of other clients the designer has worked with. Naturally, your final evaluation of a designer should always be an interview.

DESIGN MAGAZINES

Another easy way to find a designer is to look in design and decorating magazines. Find a design style that you like, find out who designed it, and contact that firm. Don't be discouraged if the design firm is not in your locale. Most designers travel to some extent. Yes, it does cost more for the designer to work out of town, but, if it's someone you really relate to, it's absolutely worth it.

AMERICAN SOCIETY OF INTERIOR DESIGNERS

The American Society of Interior Designers (ASID) has a national Web site (www.asid.org) to help you find a designer. The ASID Referral Service gives

LEFT: Nature's colors are always an excellent choice for a color scheme. It is especially true for a bedroom because of their soothing, quieting effect. *Design: Roeder Design Group; photo © 2008 by Don Pearse Photographers, Inc.*

you the names of ASID interior designers in your area. If you already have the name of a designer that you are interested in, you can search for that interior designer by name.

ASID national headquarters, located in Washington, D.C., is home to the largest professional association of interior designers, with about 19,000 practicing design members in chapters representing all of the United States and Canada. You can contact them at 202–546–3480.

ASID also has local chapters, which can be located on the national Web site. You will find designer portfolios that you can review, as well as a directory of the ASID designers in your area.

SHOWHOUSES

Visit showhouses in your area. You can often meet the designer of a space that interests you and check out an actual installation at the same time. The designer's business cards are always available at these shows, even if the designer isn't there.

NEWSPAPERS, PHONE BOOK, INTERNET

In the Home section of most local newspapers (Thursday or Sunday editions), you will find design firm ads, articles on interior design and designers, notices and reviews of showhouses, and special house and garden tours in your area. All are excellent sources for designer names and a great way to check out design styles.

Look in the Yellow Pages under *Interior Decorators and Designers* or search the Internet by entering your city, state, and "Interior Designers."

Call the interior design department of your local college or university. Often there is someone in charge of designer job referrals. Acquire a list of recommended student designers or graduates.

... it's best to have the interview in the place where the work will be done so the designer will get a feel for the space and for you, too.

The Interview

There are essentially two places to have an initial interview with a designer: your place or theirs. I always think it's best to have the interview in the place where the work will be done so the

designer will get a feel for the space and for you, too. On the other hand, if you plan to interview a number of design firms, it probably would be best to hold the interviews in the design office. It makes it easier to get an overview of the different design offices, and you will be able to maintain more objectivity when it comes time to evaluate your selections.

Having the interview at the design office is also helpful if your project is a large undertaking, since you will be able to meet the designer's staff and get a feel for the organization of the office. A large project requires a great deal of backup and support from the design office, and you should feel comfortable with the designer's team since you will ultimately be working with almost everyone on it.

WHAT A DESIGNER SHOULD HAVE AT AN INTERVIEW

» A portfolio
» List of relevant work experiences
» Client references
» Resumé with education, training, professional affiliations, and certification credentials
» The address of a current client, if possible. A project doesn't have to be fully finished for you to get a good idea of how the project is being run, the quality of the workmanship, and a general feeling for the designer's work. Many clients are sensitive about who comes onto their premises and discourage or deny visits of this nature, so this may or may not be possible for the designer to provide.

QUESTIONS TO ASK THE DESIGNER

» Can your project fit into the designer's schedule?
» Is the designer's firm available to take on your project—if not right away, then how soon?
» Can your project be finished in time to meet your deadlines or specific time frames (an open house, party, wedding)? The designer will need to meet with the other professionals involved with your project, such as an architect and

general contractor, who must then consult their schedules before a time frame for your project can be approximated.

» What can you expect for the budget? Tell the designer at this point what you have in mind for your budget. Do not be shy about talking about a budget at this early stage. Try to come up with some idea of what you think everything will cost before you arrive for the interview, or determine what you want to spend (or can afford to spend) and use that figure for your budget. You need to find out if what you want to do and the projected cost of doing it are realistic.

OTHER INTERVIEW ISSUES

How comfortable are you with the designer during the interview? Do you sense a positive attitude about your project? Does this seem like something the designer would like to do? Do you feel confident that this designer can take charge of your project? Is there any "chemistry" between you? Do you feel that a bond is being established? It is critical that you have a level of comfort at this point and are confident that this person will do his or her best for you.

Do you trust the designer? Can the designer trust you? This is probably the single most important element in the client/designer relationship. The one thing that interferes with, or even severs, a designer/client relationship is invariably a breach of trust on the part of one or the other. If you don't trust the person with whom you are working, the relationship will never go smoothly.

The Ways Designers Work

The legal document that identifies the agreement between the client and the interior designer goes by several different names: letter of agreement, proposal, acceptance letter, or contract. It serves two basic purposes: one is to define the project and determine how the designer is to be paid; the second is to protect both client and designer by making sure that the project progresses in a timely manner, that client goals are

Do you trust the designer? Can the designer trust you? This is probably the single most important element in the client/designer relationship.

met, and that timely payments are made to the design firm. When these two objectives are met, the project can move along smoothly and efficiently. These documents are covered in detail in Chapter Four.

Designers work in a variety of ways, primarily because each client and job is different, and the payment method is tailored to reflect those differences. Most designers today work with a combination of fee structures. A designer typically bases the fee arrangement on the size and complexity of the job, where the job is located, and the experience and level of expertise of the designer. The fee structures will be listed in Chapter Four.

FACING: Tastefully balanced and coordinated, the fabrics used in this guest bedroom bring a feeling of welcoming comfort to the visitor. *Design: Colleen Grace Designs; photo © 2008 by Ivy D. Photography, Inc.*

Four
Focus on Finances

The financial side of working with an interior design firm is fraught with more pitfalls than any other. You should be completely comfortable with the agreement you enter into, and it should also be one that you can live with.

A certain nervousness is completely normal initially since, in very short order, you are faced with investing large sums of money, beginning a relationship with the designer, and familiarizing yourself with the mechanics of your project. Once you start making selections, deposits, and payments, you will sense how a project flows, and you will develop a feeling for your role in the process. Your trust will deepen and you will start to relax.

Quality, Budget, and Schedule

Before you enter into a formal arrangement with a design firm, you must have firm agreement on three subjects. These are quality, budget, and schedule. Initially, there will not be enough specific details or information available to attain agreement on all three subjects. But, I can't stress enough the importance of discussing them in the initial interview, as their importance comes up early and swiftly in the project. Having a specific dollar amount established for your budget and the specific time frame in which you need to have the project done are the

two tools you need to maintain control over the proceedings.

The often-overlooked subject of quality is where both designer and client often have mismatched levels of expectation. Are you expecting a Rolls Royce or will a Subaru do very nicely at this time in your life? Are you only interested in how much something costs, and quality is not an important consideration for you? Does the designer understand this?

One of a designer's skills is to find you the best quality products within your price range. The quality may not be the best, but it's the best you can get for your budgetary level. Will that matter to you? If you have great taste and an eye and a love of quality, but it just isn't within your budget, the difference between what you want and what you can afford must be communicated to the designer.

Here is the best way to avoid misunderstandings about quality. Both of you must speak candidly about the budget. Quality is usually tied to a price tag. Price tags become your budget. A designer is trained to work with you in developing a budget and assessing your needs. Correct assessment of your needs is further defined by evaluating your quality level and your budget and by getting them synchronized. A designer is able to create a design that meets your expectations

FACING: Groups of similar objects used sparingly produce great results, as seen here in a collection of shore birds arranged on a coffee table in a seaside home. *Design: Sheridan Interiors, Inc.; photo © 2008 by Irving Solero.*

and is within your budget by knowing where to spend and where to save.

For instance, if your eyes and heart want wool, can the rest of you live with nylon carpeting? Here is where the expertise of a designer is invaluable. A designer can see alternatives where by spending less in one area—wall covering or fabric for the windows—you could afford wool carpeting. Or perhaps you both decide that nylon carpeting has a lot of advantages, and you would rather upgrade the fabric selection for the windows or spring for the cost of using a trim than spend a bundle on wool carpeting. Working with a designer is how one arrives at an informed decision. The subject must be out in the open, and your levels of expectation and the quality level you want and can afford must be clarified.

A good way to start defining your level of quality and taste is to look at samples. Almost all designers will have an ample supply of samples in their office. Ask to see comparisons of fabrics: silk, linen, cotton, polyester, wool, and blends. Let the designer explain the differences in touch, appearance, maintenance, and price. Look at samples of different woods (birch, maple, oak, walnut, mahogany, and exotics) and stains (natural, light,

> You can control the final cost of your project by clearly defining
>
> what you want and what you expect to get.

medium, and dark). Check out different types of wood finishes (pickled, lacquered, satin, high gloss, and glazed). There can be wide fluctuations in price in each of these categories.

You will undoubtedly relate to certain examples more than others. Figure out where you want to be when it comes to quality. See if there is a consistency to your choices. Let the designer help you decide a quality level for your budget. Let yourself be guided as to how and where to allocate the dollars. You can control the final cost of your project by clearly defining what you want and what you expect to get. Identify the quality that you are happiest with.

Try to get a feel for how much the designer thinks your project may cost—fifty thousand,

two hundred and fifty thousand, over five hundred thousand? You only want a general idea at this stage—don't get too specific. That will come later. Have some smelling salts on hand—it will always cost more than you expect. And take into consideration that with only a general idea of the size and scope of a project, a designer may opt to give you an answer only when the proposed work is more defined.

How Designers Set Their Fees

Below are descriptions of the different types of fee schedules that a designer might use:

» Flat fee—A fixed amount that covers payment for a specified number of services. This can range from a consultation, to creating a design concept, to providing a full, finished installation.
» Hourly rate—A set amount calculated by the hour for specified services or time spent on a project.
» Cost plus—A method of selling to the client an item or service "at cost" (meaning at the net or wholesale price), plus a percentage (specified in the client's contract) of the net cost. Items include products and furnishings; services include cabinetry and workrooms.
» Retail—The sale of items or products at the list (retail) price to the client. The designer's fee and services are covered by the difference between what the designer pays for the item (the net or wholesale price) and the retail or list price at which it is sold.
» Percentage fee—This fee arrangement is based on a percentage of the cost of the entire job or the construction costs. As a separate issue, a percentage fee can also be charged on all purchases.
» Fee based on square feet—This fee arrangement is a price per square foot based on the number of square feet of the project and is the standard method of charging used for commercial projects. The price per square foot varies

FACING: A masterful hand has very adroitly used a combination of Old World, traditional, and contemporary styling elements in this kitchen. *Design: Jamie Gibbs and Associates; photo © 2008 by Billy Cunningham.*

according to the size of the project and its complexity.

» Design fee—A fee charged for just the design of a project or space. A design fee is often based on the square footage of a job or reflects a percentage of the overall budget.

Often, a designer will request a retainer. A retainer is a fee based on a percentage of the projected cost of a project, is payable at the time of signing the letter of agreement or contract, and is retained for most of the duration of the project. A retainer serves as a form of protection for the designer during the project should there be any problem with payments. The retainer fee is credited back to the client either in partial payments as the job progresses or in full as the project nears completion.

Sometimes a designer will charge a client for the initial consultation. Prior to meeting with a designer, find out if you are being charged a fee, and if it will be credited back should the designer be hired.

If you cannot afford to hire a design firm to do your entire project, consider engaging one as a consultant. This is an economic alternative that will enable you to get the best ideas and solutions from a designer by paying an hourly fee. This way you decide how much help you need, how much you want the designer to do, and what your role in the project will be.

Real Value vs. Real Costs of a Designer

Let's evaluate the real value of an interior designer. The contract stipulates what you pay the designer, but in evaluating the real price of hiring that designer, you have to take into account the value that is added by the hidden bonuses you receive, the part that you can't put a price tag on.

Consider for a moment all the things that a designer offers or does that are not in your contract:

» The many, many valuable, practical suggestions
» The years of knowledge that lead to informed, insightful observations
» The ability to see and envision what you can't
» The ideas that come forth that wow you
» The expertise of knowing where to go to find things
» The guidance that is freely given
» A trained eye that knows when something is not right, even if you don't
» A discreet listening ear for your wish list and your desired lifestyle

These are typical skills that every designer possesses. These are values that make the difference in having a designer, along with the professional guidance that comes with the relationship, and not having one.

A Designer Can Save You Money

Looking at this from a dollars-and-cents viewpoint, you will save money having a designer. Sometimes when a designer saves you money, it's not necessarily an actual number. It's a "what I-would-have-saved-if-I-had-used-a-designer-from-the-beginning" kind of number, because it includes the time, aggravation, and worry you went through on your own. It's hard to put a price on not having stress.

A designer saves you from making costly mistakes—the ones you make when left to your own devices. How often have you gone out and purchased something, and when you brought it home it just wasn't right. You didn't solve a problem, you created another one. You have to either return the purchase or hide it somewhere. Or maybe you had something built or work done that just didn't turn out the way you wanted, but you paid good money for it, and now it is a continual reminder of a decision you wished you hadn't made, and it stares you in the face every day.

If you cannot afford to hire a design firm to do your entire project, consider engaging one as a consultant.

FACING: A master bedroom designed to be sleek and soothing is also visually engaging. *Design: Sheridan Interiors, Inc.; photo © 2008 by Wade Zimmerman, Photographer.*

You make sound informed decisions with a designer at the helm. This always saves you money. One of my clients was having an architect tear down an existing addition to her house to build a larger addition in its place. As we discussed the exterior finish of the addition, I made a suggestion that immediately—on the spot—saved her $16,000. Their initial intention was to try and match the old brick on the original section of the house, even to the point of painting and sandblasting the new brick. My suggestion was to use the same material that was on the garage, an addition on the other side of the house—cedar shingles, painted white. The two additions, in white shingles, would then flank the central brick section, making a nice balanced composition: $16,000 saved right there. They were delighted with the suggestion. Having an interior designer is an invaluable asset.

A Designer Helps You Maximize Your Home as an Investment

A designer can also help maximize the financial investment homeowners have in their residence. If you plan to resell your house or condo within a short period of time, then immediately consider hiring a designer to develop a design that is going to appeal to the unknown buyer down the line. This is different from the home-staging approach, because from the onset you are actually creating a design for the entire home with this objective in mind.

Think of your home as a "product," such as a model home or showcase. Get a design that will appeal to a broad range of people in your targeted area. Even though you will be living in it for a few years (typically one to four), depersonalize and detach yourself from the design. Pretend to be the buyer. This is how the designer thinks in this situation. That way, the two of you will make better decisions—ones that will not necessarily be for you, but ones that will make a great first impression on the prospective buyers who picture themselves living in your home.

Without a large investment, don't expect miracles, but you can at least expect a revitalized, more appealing environment. A designer can make a successful product out of your residence so that you can sell it at the highest price in the shortest amount of time. This is how you maximize your investment.

A Look at Legal Documents

Let's look at the importance and sequence of the legal documents you will be dealing with during the course of your interior design project. In the Appendix at the end of this book, you will find examples of the following documents: letter of agreement, ASID contract form, acceptance letter, proposal, floor plans, drawings, elevations, and itemized proposals/estimates.

First and foremost, in terms of importance, is the **letter of agreement** that you sign with the interior designer. It can be called a letter of agreement, acceptance letter, proposal, or contract. It is a document that sets forth the terms under which you and the designer are obligated to perform mutually-agreed-upon actions. Unless the designer is using a standard **ASID contract form,** the letter of agreement will be as individual as the designer. What designers all have in common is they will describe the areas of your project that are to be designed; the services that the design firm will provide in order to produce the designs; the methods and amount of compensation to the designer; the administrative, specifying/purchasing, and contractor management services; and payment, delivery, taxes, and termination terms.

An **acceptance letter** is an abbreviated letter of agreement. This type of agreement can be very helpful when a project is small and doesn't involve construction or building, or when there may be a question on the part of the client as to the extent of commitment made for this project. Sometimes neither client nor designer may be totally sure of the direction of a project, and an acceptance letter is a perfectly fine alternative to a letter of agreement in order to get things

Think of your home as a "product," such as a model home or showcase. Get a design that will appeal to a broad range of people in your targeted area.

started. An acceptance letter makes this arrangement very short and to the point, all the while leaving the door open for the designer or client should the project expand and both parties wish to continue the relationship.

For large residential or commercial projects, a **proposal** from a prospective design firm usually will be sent to a client when the client is interviewing several design firms. Its purpose is to interest the client and to introduce the working procedure of the design firm. After several initial meetings with the client, a proposal is presented to the client in a letter format to avoid the formality of a more structured document during the "get acquainted period." Once it has been submitted, more meetings will probably be requested to resolve various issues, but when it becomes clear that the design firm is going to be hired, then a final proposal or a letter of agreement will be prepared and submitted.

Once you have engaged an interior design firm, the first documents you will receive are **floor plans.** Floor plans may be submitted to you as individual rooms or as a full set of drawings, which will include the furniture layout of rooms, and elevations. Included in the floor plans are sheets that detail general requirements: demolition plans; drawings and plans showing new construction; electrical layouts and reflected ceiling plans; furniture floor plans and elevations; plumbing layouts and schedules; flooring, including wood and stone schedules; finish schedules (painting and wall treatments); HVAC (heating/ventilating/air-conditioning) systems; door, window and hardware schedules; as well as drawings and specifications for doors, skylights, and windows.

Elevations are drawings that show what an item will look like if you imagine looking at it straight-on where it will be located on the wall. There is no perspective in an elevation; it is a one-dimensional drawing that shows items on or against the walls as they are outlined on the floor plan. Since they are drawn to scale, you can get a clear idea of how different items in the space relate to one another. These are especially helpful in showing you where doors and windows are located and how window treatments will look, and they give you the first inkling as to what the overall design of the space will look like.

Drawings for cabinetwork, custom cabinetry, and custom furniture can be included with the floor plans but are frequently submitted later on as separate sets of drawings. It is all part of the timing involved within the design development

Once you sign off on something, it becomes a final, approved document. Any changes you want to make after this point will cost you.

phase. Once the basic design has been approved, the design team focuses next on the specialty drawings: cabinetry, custom cabinetry, custom furniture, and so forth. If your project is a large one, the sets of floor plans can contain twenty, fifty, or over a hundred pages.

Again, your signature or initials will be needed in order for work to progress. Your signature tells the designer that you have gone over every page and that you understand the information that is being conveyed. Do not become intimidated. If you don't understand something, ask to have it explained to you. If you want to change something, do it now. Once you sign off on something, it becomes a final, approved document. Any changes you want to make after this point will cost you. These are legal documents and you need to understand the seriousness of your commitment.

These documents also serve to protect you. This is your guarantee that what has been proposed will be delivered. It is a two-way street. For your part, you need to view and comprehend the drawings. This is the best way for you to make sure things do turn out looking like the drawing. Another form of protection is to ask the designer if you can make a "progress check" on the item—whether it is cabinetry, custom furniture, or window treatments. Visit the cabinet shop or workroom to see how things are shaping up. You can get an idea of what the item is intended to look like, even if it is only partway finished. If you are unsure or unhappy

FACING: The attraction of opposites demonstrates the dramatic effects of high/low ceiling heights and light/dark color schemes in the library adjacent to a living room. *Design: RSB Interiors; photo © 2008 by Ivy D. Photography, Inc.*

about the way it looks, course corrections can still be made at this stage.

Sometimes things don't turn out looking like the drawing. Go back to the drawings and double check what you are looking at. Consult with the designer if something does not look the way you expected. Mistakes do happen. On occasion style/model numbers, price), and the delivery address of where it is being shipped. The P.O., as it is generally referred to, usually includes a deposit or full payment to the vendor, and the signature of a person in the design office authorized to place orders. This is a legal document for the designer. Any mistakes that occur with this order are proved

You may be in a position to trade or barter with the designer. This can be a beneficial arrangement for both sides.

it may be necessary to make accommodations to the design. You should be informed as soon as your designer becomes aware of any changes that must be made. On every project there will always be unknown things that happen and site conditions that necessitate changes; as a result, there are always "extras." If you expect overages during the course of your project, you are less likely to be upset by any unexpected occurrences. Factor in that your project will come in at 10 to 20 percent higher than the predicted budget, and you will be prepared for any "surprises" that may happen.

Once items or services are ready to be ordered, you will be sent the itemized **proposal** or **estimate**. The two terms are interchangeable and mean the same thing: an item or service is proposed, estimated, and presented to you for your consideration. It contains a description of the item or service to be performed, the cost of said item or service, and a request for (usually) a 50 percent deposit. You will be asked to sign this document, signifying your approval to have the designer purchase the item or service for you, and pay the deposit. One signed copy of the estimate and the deposit are then returned to the design office. The remaining balance is due when you are invoiced by the design firm.

Often a proposal or estimate will be accompanied by a drawing or elevation, and these, too, will need your initials or signature to signify your approval to have the designer implement the work or order the product.

Purchase orders are documents that are created in the designer's office. They describe an item(s) or a service to be purchased, all pertinent information needed to order it (such as color, or disproved with the information (or lack of) on the designer's purchase order. This is a very serious document for the designer.

Change orders are documents that originate from the contractor. Any time the client or designer wants a change in the plans, or something occurs in the field that necessitates a change in the floor plans or drawings, and the contractor has to do something different or in addition to his signed-off plans, he charges for it. The change order is submitted first to the design office to authorize the change and approve the price the contractor is charging for it. Then it is submitted to the client for payment. Change orders are put through with the express consent of the client and the designer. If you do not feel that the change order is correct, talk to your designer about it. Come to an agreement, and then, if necessary, have the designer speak to the contractor.

Paying the Designer

Most designers have set policies regarding their design fees and how they bill, and they will not negotiate the terms of their contract. If you ask for a deal or a bargain price and the answer is no, simply accept that the designer has very definite reasons for charging that price and that, in the end, you will get what you pay for. You either hire this firm on the designer's terms or not.

You may be in a position to trade or barter with the designer. This can be a beneficial arrangement for both sides. One designer I know, in return for a lower fee for his work on

ABOVE: Accessories provide lots of style for this home office—tribal arts objects as well as Oriental pieces are used in an original display. *Design: DCA Design Inc; photo © 2008 by Michael Mahovlich Photography.*

a hotel, worked out an arrangement where he occasionally gets a free room plus discounts on the use of conference and reception rooms. This is the perfect solution for him for his frequent out-of-town guests, and he has a place to entertain as well as hold meetings.

You may still choose to counteroffer what the designer has proposed. The designer may agree to your offer so the job isn't lost altogether. Later on, when the job is underway, the designer may have the feeling of having made a bad deal. You do not want a designer in that frame of mind. You want someone who is thrilled to be working for you and is fully engaged in your project. Conversely, if this is someone that you really want to work with, are you prepared to blow it? Many designers categorically refuse to work with someone who insists on bargaining.

Deciding to work with an interior designer is a decision to make an investment. As you would with any investment, choose carefully. It will bear interest in the value that the designer adds. It will have a big return if you are patient, anticipate highs and lows, and consistently consult with your investment adviser, your designer.

Five

Contrary to what many people believe, interior design is not some mysterious activity based on secret machinations known only to a talented few. Although it is very complimentary to hear someone describe a space transformation as "magical," that is the designer's skill: to take ideas and orchestrate and organize them into a design. Designers don't think of what they do as either mysterious or magical. They say, "It's what we do."

The process of creating interior design is amazingly involved and depends on highly detailed decision-making. It takes huge amounts of time to complete the design process: design it, execute it, and get it right. Design is not based on the wave of a magic wand.

In fact, design is a process of specific, predetermined phases, implemented by defined tasks. It is important to have a clear idea of how the design process unfolds and to become familiar with the process and the different phases of a project. As you gain insight into the design process, you will see why the process takes the time it does and the amount of detail it entails.

Analyzing the Interior Design Process

PRE-DESIGN/PROGRAMMING PHASE

In this initial phase, the interior designer determines the objectives of the design problem. Discussion centers around "what do you want to do?" The functions of the space (what you want to do in the space) are explored, defined, and slated to be designed. In this phase, any special requirements that you want are discussed and included in the "to be designed" list. Also up for discussion are your resources and limitations, which include human, physical, and financial ones.

In the pre-design phase, any existing documents are reviewed. These include original floor plans, drawings, specifications, lease agreements, etc. The existing conditions of the project are reviewed, zoning requirements are noted, and research is conducted for applicable building codes. Then spatial relationships are explored and analyzed, including adjacencies, traffic flow, etc. The programming of the project is underway.

SCHEMATIC/CONCEPTUAL DESIGN PHASE

The actual design process is begun in this phase by the design office. Preliminary design directions are established for character, style, and three-dimensional design. Space planning is

FACING: This tiniest of powder rooms is visually expanded by adding a full-height mirror on one wall and using a serene Oriental style for the decór. Luxury touches include the onyx stone basin and floor. *Design: Sheridan Interiors, Inc.; photo © 2008 by Irving Solero.*

are prepared: floor plans and elevations; reflected ceiling and electrical plans; furniture and fixture plans; drawings of details and sections; specifications; perspective/axonometric drawings; presentation boards; and art, accessories, graphics/signage, and interior plantscaping programs. The requirements stated in the pre-design phase are verified and updated. The involvement of outside consultants is coordinated. The client again gives signed approval.

CONTRACT DOCUMENTS PHASE

The contract documents referred to here are the ones that are submitted to general contractors, workrooms, installers, and relevant consultants for bidding and negotiation. These are generated by the interior designer's office and may include: working drawings; specifications for interior construction; general and special conditions to the contract; reflected ceiling and electrical/voice/data plans; elevations; specifications of furniture, fixtures, and equipment; finish schedules; and furniture, fixture, and equipment drawings. Outside consultants' contract documents (drawings and specifications) are reviewed and coordinated. Appropriate construction documents are prepared for permit applications to obtain required building or governmental approvals.

All contract and bid documents are prepared in compliance with relevant codes and building rules and regulations to ensure the health, safety, and welfare of the client.

Bidding documents are issued to qualified bidders to facilitate the bidding process and to receive proposals.

PURCHASING PHASE

Purchases and services for resale to the client are proposed by the designer. After receiving client approval, purchase orders are prepared and issued by the designer as the client's agent. Client invoices for specified products or services on the purchase orders are prepared and presented for payment.

CONTRACT ADMINISTRATION PHASE

This phase is intensive for the designer, and the client sees the work progress. The following is a

begun and layouts are established for furniture, furnishings, and equipment. At this point, probable costs can be determined. Materials, furnishings, color, and finishes are selected. Building/environmental systems or issues are reviewed. Preliminary presentation materials are prepared. Outside consultants are contacted and their involvement is coordinated. The requirements stated in the pre-design phase are verified and updated. You, the client, give signed approval for the design direction.

DESIGN DEVELOPMENT PHASE

It is in the design development phase where the designer starts to pull everything together. Now the activities in the conceptual design phase are refined and finalized: design concepts; space planning; furniture, furnishings, and equipment layouts; as well as the selection of materials, furnishings, colors, and finishes. Estimated costs become specific and a budget is established.

In this phase, all of the official design development documents and presentation materials

RIGHT: A sunny, open-air loggia has a surprise pair of lusciously full taffeta curtains that forms an intimate room setting by concisely defining a sitting area. *Design: Giovanni Naso Designs; photo © 2008 by Ivy D. Photography, Inc.*

Starting Design Development

tick list of what the designer will do for the client in this stage:

» Collect bids, make recommendations to the client to contract for construction and installation, and assist the client in preparation of contractor/owner contract(s). Review shop drawings, samples, and submittals to ensure compliance with contract documents and design concept.
» Review contractors' schedules and coordinate with consultants, contractors, and vendors by attending project meetings.
» Make regular site visits to monitor adherence to contract documents.
» Facilitate decision-making regarding changes to the contract documents and communicate with everyone with appropriate documentation.
» Provide ongoing administration to ensure that completion of the project is in compliance with the contract documents, that it is within the budget, and that it is on schedule.
» Review and approve contractors' requests for payment.
» Oversee the installation of furniture, furnishings, equipment, and materials.
» Prepare punch lists and/or reports to record incomplete or substandard construction and installation.
» Assist in distributing warranties, manuals, record (as-built) drawings, certificates of completion, and other necessary documentation to the appropriate parties in order to close out the project.

POST-OCCUPANCY EVALUATION

A post-occupancy evaluation is a review of the project with the client to assess the success of the project.

By surveying and observing, the designer will determine if the project program and requirements were met, if the client's goals and objectives were met, and if the design team's goals and objectives were met. The post-occupancy evaluation findings will be documented, analyzed, and reported, and the issues raised will be addressed by the designer.

As you can see, the path a project follows must be very detailed and specific for it to conclude successfully. Use of the Analysis of the Interior Design Process in the Appendix will help you understand the process, anticipate what happens next, and keep you from feeling lost or muddled by the amount of work entailed. With a good designer and team, you can be realistically assured of a happy, successful outcome.

Defining Your Style

By now you should have come to certain decisions about the style in which you want to live. We talked about how a designer can help in developing your style in Chapter One. Ultimately you are the one who is making the decisions and ticking off the final approvals. These decisions will be with you for an extended period of time. Once you arrive at the point in the design process where you are approving plans and furnishings, you need to be fully confident of the direction in which the design is going. You need to feel that this is the style for you.

To define your design style is to define your lifestyle: how you see yourself living. Here is a little exercise to help clarify your thinking. Imagine yourself answering the door and greeting guests as they arrive for a cocktail party, dinner party, special luncheon, children's birthday party, holiday celebration, or Sunday brunch. What do you see? What is the outfit you are wearing? Do you see the room that you are in—what color is it? Do you get a feeling for the furnishings? Can you put a name to the style? Does it match the style that the designer is presenting to you?

Maybe you have no intention of entertaining, but you do want special surroundings for yourself. What are you doing in this setting and how are you dressed? Do you plan to cook, work on hobbies, or have a home office? Is this a private getaway? Is it a second home for extended family get-togethers involving seasonal activities? It is important to have a style because this is your life and you are the most important person in it. Live

To define your design style is to define your lifestyle: how you see yourself living.

it well and in comfort, surrounded with things that you really enjoy.

In order for your project to move along smoothly, you need to know what you want or, at the very least, know what you don't like. You want to avoid time-consuming periods of having to reshop or start all over when it comes to the design of your project. If the choices your designer is making are not making you happy, organize your thoughts as to why and what it is you are not relating to, and talk it over with the designer. You and the designer need to be on the same wavelength. Review your initial choices and see if the selections match up with what is being selected for you now. If there are changes in your design direction or taste level, clarify that with the designer and redefine the direction the designer should take.

Take the time to be sure about your decisions, but first, be sure of where your style is headed. I enjoy working with one couple so much because the woman is so open about her likes and dislikes, and she lets me know what they are. Yet, at the same time, she really listens to my suggestions

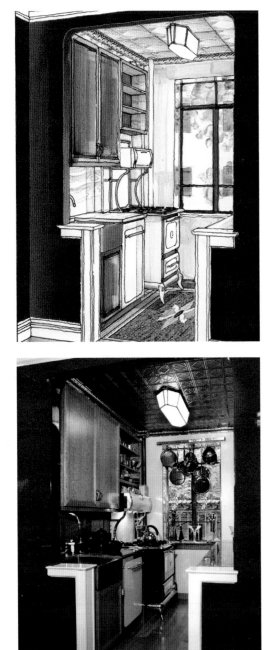

and evaluates them. I can see the wheels turning as we talk. Initially, they both seemed to want a contemporary look to their apartment, with the husband not wanting anything that looked like it "belonged to his grandmother." She wanted different, unexpected elements and was passionate about gold-leaf finishes. As we worked together, their taste level turned more and more to French-style furniture, especially Louis XVI. Their design preferences have now evolved into a truly eclectic style that is an exciting mix of contemporized traditional upholstered pieces with a scattering of authentic-looking Louis XVI pieces in (real) gold-leaf finishes, all of which are sitting on a magnificent twenty-first-century silk and wool rug. Their place looks fabulous. It reflects their exuberance, their openness to experience life, their love of having really nice things—it is their lifestyle.

For you to be happy with the end result, you have to agree with selections that are being made as the project evolves. Pay attention to the direction that the color, furniture styles, fabrics, and finishes are taking. Don't wait until the sofa has been delivered to say, "I never really liked that fabric."

Here is another "don't." Don't select items randomly. You may wind up with schemes that don't work. But if that happens, a designer is invaluable. He or she can help you pull together seemingly incompatible choices and get the whole thing to look as if it were always meant to be that way.

Look at magazines, check out furniture styles on the Internet, go to showrooms, invest the time it takes to thoroughly research your color preferences, and then, when you and your designer make choices, know that this is the best you can do for the moment. Three years from now, you may change your mind again. On the other hand, I have a client who wanted me to find and replace the same fabric she chose twenty years ago for her sofa and matching loveseat.

Visualizing a Project

One of the worst things for a designer to hear is "This isn't what I was expecting!" when something has just been delivered or installed. The designer is anticipating "Oh, it's beautiful! It looks just like I thought it would!" This disparity in expectations happens for several reasons. Sometimes the client didn't really comprehend the drawing or floor plans that were presented. Other times the client couldn't envision how much impact a fabric, a wall color, or a wood finish would have in a room when all they had seen was a small sample. And some clients are simply unable to envision what an item is going to look like until it's actually been delivered and/or installed.

UNDERSTANDING DRAWINGS AND FLOOR PLANS

One way a designer can help the client understand drawings and floor plans is to create the concept two-dimensionally. Looking at floor plans or drawings is a one-dimensional experience. Clients may become confused trying to understand floor plans or elevations, and they don't want to admit it.

Designers often use a simple technique to help a client understand how a piece will look in the space. Using masking tape or chalk, they tape or draw an outline on the floor that represents the actual size and location of a sofa, chair, bed, table, or cabinetry in the room. They can tape or draw chalk lines on the walls to represent a mirror, painting, large cabinetry or wall unit, and even drapery. They can show a client visually how wide a chandelier will be and how far down it will extend. They can convey with a measuring tape just where a bedpost or a refrigerator will be in the space. A designer might even make accurately dimensioned paper cutouts of lampshades and hold them up in the space. This way a client can "see" how big or small the lampshade will be.

In large spaces it is often necessary to provide full-scale mock-ups of window treatments. The drapery workroom will make this in muslin, and the swags, valance, or draperies can be held up in place. You get an idea of how the window

ABOVE: A rendering of a proposed kitchen makeover made for the presentation to the client, and below, the finished project. *Design and rendering: Terry Stewart Interior Design; photo © 2008 by Font New York, Ltd.*

FACING: A perfectly balanced furniture arrangement complemented by finely detailed upholstery and window treatment details make this living room most inviting. *Design: Roeder Design Group; photo © 2008 by Don Pearse Photographers, Inc.*

treatment will look when finished, and it is easy for the designer to tell if adjustments need to be made.

Chandeliers in grand rooms are traditionally big-ticket items. For this reason alone, the design office will often make a full mock-up of a chandelier and put it in position in order for everyone to see it before it is purchased. The designer makes the "chandelier" out of foam core, cut to the basic shape and accurately dimensioned. It's a lot easier to do it this way than to bring in the very heavy, very expensive real chandelier and try to hold it in place. But that could be an option as well.

Sometimes the best way to get a client over the hurdle of visualizing what a room or an aspect of a room will look like is to provide a three-dimensional drawing of it. An artist specializing in room renderings (as they are called) does this for an additional fee. A CADD (computer aided design and drafting) rendering can also be generated as an additional service. A color rendering

FACING: The designer's ideas for a music room as presented to the client in a rendering. *Design and rendering: Terry Stewart Interior Design.*

ABOVE: An upstairs hall is just the right size for the music room and is a perfect location from which to send music throughout the house. *Design: Terry Stewart Interior Design; photo © 2008 by Phillip Ennis Photography.*

in three-dimension can make all the difference in conveying what a room design will look like.

USING SAMPLES

Color is an important element in any project. It is also the area that can be potentially disruptive to you when you see a large amount of it in your space. The designer should get the largest sample of a fabric, paint color, or cabinetry panel that is available so that you understand the impact these materials will have in a space. A showroom will often loan out the wing sample of a selected fabric to the designer for a few hours so that it can be taken to the project site.

Wall-covering firms will sometimes loan a "test" sample of their product, or your designer might just buy a large piece of covering or even a roll. The clarity and impact of the wall covering is inescapable when a large piece is right in front of you.

The designer can also arrange with the painter to paint large samples of the wall color on a good-sized piece of cardboard or Masonite or, ideally, on a wall in the space. Seeing a large swath of color on the wall really helps you decide if this is a color you can live with. Color is always an emotional subject.

If you have a hard time visualizing, even when drawings, large samples, and mock-ups are pro-

vided, you probably turned to a designer for that very reason. In this scenario, both you and the designer have to have trust and confidence in the other. If you have that kind of trust, then just forge ahead.

However, if you don't have a trusting relationship already established, I suggest that you have the designer design and install just one room. It's more expensive to do things this way, but in the long run it will save you, the client, money. If you don't like the style and design once you see it in one room, you can stop and reassess the situation. If you do like it, you can speed forth with the rest of the job.

Considering Your Ideas vs. Their Ideas

If you have a designer who is very strong about keeping the design, it is probably because that designer has a signature look, a style that is easily identifiable. The designer's style was most likely the reason you hired that person. Allow the designer the right to maintain his or her own style. In the end you will have a design that is that designer's signature, but be prepared to live with what the designer has selected for you. A lot of designers that fall into this camp refuse

The Intensity of Color

One of my earliest clients was a beautiful, redheaded actress. I designed her living room with apricot walls and blue and white fabrics and accessories. She had moved out for the duration of the project, and I was bubbling with excitement on the day she came to see the painted living room.

One look, and she became hysterical. She didn't just hate the apricot walls, she detested them! I was shocked. I knew she would look stunning in that apricot room. What had happened? I talked her into waiting until the furnishings were in the room, and, if she was still unhappy, we would change the color.

Once she saw the finished room, she absolutely loved it! She looked and felt as if she were on a television set designed for her. This is a frequent occurrence. A painted room with nothing in it can look harsh and glaring. If someone has been living with white walls, for example, the switch to a color can be traumatizing. Color becomes much more saturated and intense in an empty room, and one can have a very adverse reaction seeing it in large amounts for the first time.

to make any changes to their original selections. They insist that in the end you will love it, and most likely you will. Just make sure from the beginning that this is the designer you really want, whose work you really like, because that is what you are going to get. If you still want a say in the proceedings, get up your courage and remind the designer of the first cardinal rule in design, "I'm the one who has to live with it, not you."

What about the designers whose styles are more flexible? Does this mean they don't have a style? Far from it. It may mean that their style is more subtle, and that there is a greater range to their style repertoire. I like to compare this type of designer to a good actor who can play a wide variety of roles. Having this type of designer usually means having a more collaborative relationship. Both of you are participating in the process, and each of you contributes different ideas to explore, with the designer taking the lead in making evaluations and final decisions.

Designers should not back down if they know that they are right. On a recent renovation of a living room, one of the changes I insisted upon was that it needed crown moulding. The client was adamantly against it; she felt it was money wasted. I was adamantly for it; I knew the room just wouldn't look right without it. Thankfully, the client bowed to my expertise, and the moulding was installed. It is perfect—a classic egg and dart design. The client confessed one day that the one thing she loves most in the new living room is the crown moulding! When you sense that the designer is not going to budge on an issue, go with the designer's choice.

If you have very specific ideas about what you want and are only interested in having your ideas executed, you need to be very up front when you approach designers. Tell them that you want to have your ideas and designs executed as is. If you want only their expertise and guidance, and perhaps suggestions, and you want them to place the orders and make sure everything gets installed, tell them. As long as you are up front with your plan, you will find many designers who are willing to work this way.

One of my clients had basic concepts for the window designs and fabric choices, and she wanted a designer who could take the designs and turn them into window treatments. Her designs were extremely original. Although I was the person who drew it all up, organized it, and dealt with the workroom, in the end it was her designs that became the installed window treatments, and they are stunning.

If you remain flexible and are willing to accept new ideas, your design experience will be invigorating, and you will learn a great deal in the process. Flexibility is the key to a successful design venture. Are you flexible enough to let a designer have the final say? Are you flexible in listening to new ideas, in considering unexpected colors, in looking at different styles? Can you be open and receptive to designs that, at first glance, may seem bizarre or "not you"? Listen to the designer's ideas. The ideas may produce a spontaneous response in you. Be up front and verbalize what you are thinking. It's so important to communicate. Reticence in speaking up will be a disservice to you and the designer.

Talk things over, turn the ideas inside out, and maybe the resulting solution will be a combination of your ideas, a compromise, or a new idea entirely. Don't close the door on a new and different way of looking at something just because it's unfamiliar. Take some time to let the new idea percolate. Given a day or two, you may find yourself really excited by this unexpected, "bizarre" suggestion. It may open up a part of you that you never knew existed. Part of the role of being a client is to experience the unexpected; otherwise you could have just stayed where you have always been, with the "expected." You wouldn't have needed or wanted to look to a designer for help.

Working with a designer can bring out a lot of issues in a client that previously went unnoticed and unchallenged. Most of them integrate successfully into the new designer/client relationship, as everyone finds the way to get what they want. It really is all about getting what you want and what the designer thinks is right. How one goes about this is the key to the success of the relationship.

If you remain flexible and are willing to accept new ideas, your design experience will be invigorating, and you will learn a great deal in the process.

For people who need to be in control, working with a designer who must be in control can be quite troublesome. Many people are used to running a house, a business, or a family. Many people are *not* used to someone else making decisions, speaking authoritatively, or giving orders to them.

If you are a self-described control freak, you could find yourself having issues with a designer. There may be times on the project when you will say, "This is what I want, this is how I want it installed, and this is where it's going to go!" And your designer will know that that is the end of the matter. The designer is not the one who is going to live there.

If you insist on your way over the opinion of the designer, the final result winds up in one of three ways. You may end up with something not all that bad, and the designer may even (grudgingly) admit it. You may convince yourself that you made a good choice even though you are the only one who thinks so. Or, you may realize you made a bad decision, whether you ever admit it out loud or not. Everyone moves on. It's not the end of the world.

It is hard for a person used to making all the decisions to give up control over what seems to be a very important aspect of life. Get rid of the idea that you are giving up anything. You aren't. The person making decisions here is simply the person who is best qualified for this particular domain. Give that person the freedom to be the expert that you hired in the first place. You would

> Couples can be very much a team and agree on almost everything as we proceed, or they can have a hard time reaching agreement on almost anything. A good way to handle this is to let the designer make final decisions.

expect to have the same freedom if the situation were reversed, wouldn't you? If you really are unhappy about something and don't like it, it can always be changed.

Listening to Other Opinions

Everybody loves to show others what they are doing in the home decorating area. People love to pull out floor plans and color schemes with all the samples and show them to anyone who comes along—children, Mom and Dad, aunts, friends, in-laws, and even doormen. It is always interesting to hear what other people have to say, but their opinions are simply their opinions. Be gracious and say thank you to opinions that are offered, but leave your designer out of this scenario. In the end, your opinions are the only ones that matter.

People ask for others' opinions mostly for reassurance and, occasionally, to settle a question about one of the choices. There is nothing wrong with this as long as you keep things in perspective. Don't expect your designer to change the design because you say that your doorman says the blue stripe fabric doesn't go with the rest of the fabrics (I actually had this happen). If you feel compelled to relay the opinion of your doorman to your designer, then say, "You won't believe what my doorman thinks about this blue stripe fabric!" The designer, upon receiving this cue from you, might look again at the blue stripe and reconsider it. Or then again, you might get a look, a pause, and a firm "It's fine."

Your designer is the professional, and although your mother-in-law may have good intentions, her opinion is that of a layperson. Ask yourself how her opinion could be more valid than that of your designer's. Should you run into stiff opposition on something, just say, "I hired a professional designer to help me with this, and this is the choice we have made. I am happy with it."

Couples can be very much a team and agree on almost everything as we proceed, or they can have a hard time reaching agreement on almost anything. A good way to handle this is to let the designer make final decisions. That way neither partner is responsible for a decision, and the designer can always be blamed if the result is unfavorable, letting the other partner off the hook.

Sometimes one partner backs down (and may even walk off) if things don't go the way that he or she wants. A designer can usually see early on that this is the pattern of how things get worked out in their relationship; the design can proceed in the right direction without the designer taking sides.

Teamwork is the ideal state for the design process. The designer works best if both partners are interested in what the space is going to look like and both actively participate in making decisions. And it is best to have both people giving their opinions directly to the designer rather than having one speak for an absentee partner. Your decisions should be made with the person you have hired to help you.

Matters of Taste

The matter of taste is a delicate issue. It is also truly a personal issue, yet a surprising number of people think they can just go out and buy it. The more expensive something is, they think, the greater the guarantee that it will be in good taste. Others figure that if they like something, that's all that matters—then they can say, that's my taste. Some things money cannot buy, and taste is one of them.

Many people don't really know what they like, or they don't have an "eye" for design, or they don't know what direction to go in. Unsure about their own taste level, they turn to a name or a brand they have heard of, to something that someone has said is "in," to something they saw on TV; or they let themselves be talked into buying something that they are told is "just right" for them. They buy it and, before long, they wind up with a house full of things that do not work together. To make matters worse, they usually have spent a great deal of money doing this.

If this is how you feel or if this has happened to you, you are someone who needs to be working with a professional designer, who, if not making these decisions for you, is at least guiding you in your selections. Make sure that the person you choose to work with has a taste level that you relate to and is one in whom you have complete confidence.

Designers will usually try to clue you in if you have something that they think should be changed. Maybe they will say that the object has seen better days, or that it is time for a change. Maybe they will say that it might look better in a different location, or you might consider having the object reupholstered. Listen carefully. They are tactfully telling you that, no matter how much you paid for that object, it just doesn't belong.

With couples, differences of taste can be vast. You may prefer traditional styles, while your spouse can't bear anything that remotely resembles traditional and only likes contemporary. In a good, established relationship, how you handle this in your life has been worked out long before the designer comes onto the scene. When you call upon a designer, it is more a question of finding help in how to integrate your preferences into the same space rather than needing help in dealing with your differences. You already know how to live with your differences.

In case of an impasse, one of you is usually more inclined to give in and go with the other partner's choice. When one partner's preferences are clearly known, they usually take precedence. A client might say, "Charles would definitely not like that . . . let's go with this chair instead." If one partner needs to be convinced of an idea, the designer will often stay out of it and leave the convincing up to the other partner. Sometimes the resolution of differences is best worked out as a compromise. If the subject is about style, and you like yellow and Louis XVI furniture, but your spouse likes red and clean-lined contemporary furnishings, the designer will probably use the colors and styles in separate rooms: yellow/French in the living room and red/contemporary in the den. When the differences are in the same room—for instance, the accessories and artwork—you and your partner must eventually agree on some level and reach a communal agreement that everyone can live with.

LEFT: Look at the interesting mix of blues in the fabrics, lavender on the walls and vase, and the light woods for the furniture and cabinetry. All together this updated dining room says "designed for today's living." *Design: Markham Interiors; photo © 2008 by Judith Fox.*

Working with an interior designer on a project is many things, but most of all it's a learning experience. If you have a partner, you learn patience and compromise. If you are doing this solo, you learn patience and compromise. Here is the second cardinal rule of design: things always work out. The trick is getting them worked out so that you are happy.

The design development process can and should be fun. Do not allow yourself to get bogged down with the time it takes to get something done or discouraged when things are not going

Design is a great adventure: it's discovering all the possibilities, all the ways in which something can be done . . .

well. It will be over before you know it. Design is a great adventure: it's discovering all the possibilities, all the ways in which something can be done, and all the things you never knew about. Allow yourself to get swept up in the process and really enjoy the proceedings, because you are going to love the outcome.

Six

Dealing with the Budget

As work on your project progresses, you will be getting proposal after proposal for items that are to be ordered. As you add up the items, you are, in effect, finalizing your budget.

There are two things to take into account about a design and decorating budget: the first is that it will always be higher than you expected, and the second is that it will keep changing (make that increasing). It's just the way life is. It's the same with buying a car. You pick one that seems pretty reasonable and then you decide to add a few "extras," and what started out as a very affordable Mazda has suddenly turned into a Cadillac. We always want the best and the most, and when we get the bill it's a bit of a jolt. So, what do you do?

Paying for Your Projects

COST AVERAGING

There are several ways to handle the financial end of your design project. One way is to use a cost-averaging technique. If you want some expensive things, then cut back on other items so that when you total everything up, the figure for the budget will average out or be close to the one that you started with. Use this technique for a room, the construction budget, or the whole project.

Let's say you plan to spend $50,000 to furnish the living room, but you have your heart set on a carpet that uses up one-third of your budget.

Now you need to cut back on other items in the budget so that the bottom line will average out close to your original figure. Identify your other "big ticket" items in the budget, such as a built-in wall unit or cabinetry, painting/papering, window treatment, and sofa. Your designer will help you look at ways to cut back in these areas. You might need to pare down the design of the wall unit; use paint on the walls instead of a wall covering; go to a retail furnishings company instead of a posh showroom for well-designed, well-made furniture; or shop for fabric and trim bargains at discount stores, closeouts, and warehouse sales.

This type of cost averaging is really a balancing act, and no one is better at it than your designer. The knowledge and experience of a designer can save you a lot of money. What is it worth to you to get the look you want for a realistic price within a realistic time frame? Let the designer struggle with the decisions that will get your budget to work.

PAYING IN INSTALLMENTS

Don't focus on the total of what something is going to cost. If it is really something that you want, bear in mind that you will be living with it for some time, and then ask yourself what it is worth over a ten- or twenty-year period? Do you want it badly enough to pay for it in installments?

Many purchases are broken up into two payments: a 50 percent deposit upon ordering and

FACING: Steeped in the aura of authentic Americana accessories, this charming living room expresses a clear-eyed interpretation of American style. *Design: Room Service Design, Inc.; photo © 2008 by Phillip Ennis Photography.*

the balance due on delivery. Furniture can take three, four, even six months for delivery, and a custom rug can take close to a year. A two-payment plan makes it easier to allocate your funds and also allows you the luxury of considering something you might decide against because of the price.

Cabinetry and construction are both long-term investments. With cabinetwork, the payment process is often divided into three or four payments. It is the size of the contract or proposal that makes this determination: the larger the contract or proposal, the more deposits and payments. With construction agreements, payments are usually made with an initial deposit of a third or half, and the balance paid in several subsequent payments. Stretching your funds out this way can make all the difference in your buying decisions. Even though you might wait for installations and orders, it gives you a little breathing room in the payment process.

THE LAYAWAY PLAN

Another method of payment is what I call the layaway plan. You have everything designed and selected, but you don't do everything all at once. You allocate purchases into phases. Look at the overall amount of work you have planned. Separate what you have planned into big, medium, and small financial expenditures. For example, the first year you may make major repairs and/or alterations or do as much as your budget will allow. The next year you finish the ceilings, walls, and floors, including the bathrooms and kitchen. The third year, you work on furniture and fabrics, and so forth. To get the layaway plan to work successfully, you must have a fully developed set of plans, even if they are not totally finished at the outset. All rooms should be laid out; and the lighting, electrical, and furniture floor plans should be finalized. Although furniture pieces and fabrics don't have to be selected for a while, you will still need to develop a color palette in order to decide colors of floor finishes, stone selections, and tiles. These decisions occur in the early phases of the project and, once made, will keep you locked into a color scheme, so be very sure of your choices.

> A professionally designed space is pulled together. There is thought and coherence behind the design. With few exceptions, designing without the aid of a professional will never give you the same polished results.

Getting the Most of Your Investment

Look at the budget issue from a different slant. You have a budget—a good-sized one—of $250,000. You already know it's not enough for what you want to do. But that is your limit. Do you still commit to doing the project? My answer is, yes—you can't lose. Even though some of that money will go toward paying for a designer, you will get a design that looks as if it cost twice as much—$500,000. What does a designer do that can so dramatically affect the final outcome?

First and foremost, it will be D-E-S-I-G-N-E-D by a professional designer. A professionally designed space is pulled together. There is thought and coherence behind the design. With few exceptions, designing without the aid of a professional will never give you the same polished results.

Take the cabinetry part of your project—usually a sizable chunk of the budget. Instead of using mahogany or walnut, a designer can suggest woods that are less expensive yet look fabulous when stained and finished. A skilled faux-finish painter can paint doors, trim, and crown mouldings to look like wood or marble. Craftsmen who specialize in woodworking can be engaged to copy antique pieces. These are all strong elements in the design of a space that can make it look much more expensive than it costs.

What about floors? There are porcelain or ceramic tiles that are made to look like stone. Your designer can save you a bundle in giving you a faux-stone floor. Wall coverings as a rule are more expensive to use than paint because of cost and installation. But a wall covering will last longer than paint, is often easier to clean, and protects the wall. Plus it brings a unique quality to a room—depth, texture, warmth, and atmosphere; there's no denying it makes a room special.

There are wall coverings that emulate faux finishes, and then there are the faux finishes. Whether using paint or a wall covering will be more economical depends on what style or pattern you have in mind—how complicated is the faux finish, how many colors does it require? The cost of a specific wall-covering product can vary widely as can the rates of the installer. Painted

LEFT: Here lighting transforms a hallway into a dramatic, unforgettable passageway. *Design: Room Service Designs, Inc.; photo © 2008 by Phillip Ennis Photography.*

stripes are very effective both visually and economically, and you get a truly unique design with this technique. Again, there are ways to add to the illusion that something looks much more expensive than it actually is.

Accessorizing also serves to separate the professionally finished space from one that is not. Store vignettes, show house installations, model homes and apartments all look good because they are accessorized.

Unfortunately, when a client gets close to the end of a project and it's time for the accessorizing, usually one of two things happens: either there is no money left in the coffers (because of cost overruns in other areas) or the client feels that he or she will use what's left of the budget and do the accessorizing themselves. Then the client flounders in a vast sea of too much product, too many choices, and not enough confidence to put it together.

Interestingly, accessorizing is not that easy for a lot of designers. Some designers specialize in it; others do very little. It takes a well-trained eye to accessorize a space well and it takes money,

Dealing with the Budget

sometimes a lot. Certain avenues can yield great finds without forcing you to take out another loan. At the top of my list for all types of accessories are Pottery Barn, Pier One, and Crate and Barrel. I find well-designed, well-priced accessories at these stores. I haunt garage sales, house sales, and estate sales. Auction prices usually escalate beyond my budget, but there are flea markets, sidewalk vendors, "nearly new" shops, antiques and collectibles stores and stalls, and secondhand shops to be explored.

Staying in Your Budget

How can you keep the spending on track and still keep the budget on target? Try to keep an overview of the proceedings in your head. Plan on dividing your budget into percentages. These numbers will vary depending on the size and type of project you have. But, generally speaking, for a renovation/redecoration project, nearly half of your budget will be going to construction and cabinetwork. Allow another 40 percent for the design and decorating and the last 10 percent for accessorizing.

If you see one section of your budget requiring ever-greater amounts of money, with the threat of undermining the whole budget, pull back. Put certain things on hold. Say no to a more expensive finish or custom tile. Cost overruns in the construction part of a project can eat up a client's entire budget. It is very difficult to say no to the many beautiful choices that you are offered, but put it into perspective. When the trade is a more expensive item versus a finished space . . . which would you rather have in the long run?

Keep within the percentages you have set up in advance. Keep checking and revising the figures as new ones come in or established ones change. When you see things getting closer and closer to your limit, and you know there are more purchases to be made, sit down and talk it over with your designer and/or your contractor. There are always less expensive substitutes that can be made in any category. Everyone would rather have a fully finished project instead of one with empty rooms, bare windows, and acres of gorgeous marble floors.

Dealing with Cost Overruns

Site conditions are the biggest culprits of cost overruns. Unfortunately, they usually cannot be bartered or traded up or down, and they often affect other areas of the design. Think about the real cost of making adjustments at this point in the design process. Do not be pressured into making decisions on the spot. Remember, it is a job site, and if you want another opinion, take the time to get it.

Bigger, better, and custom are other areas of cost escalation. A bigger plasma screen is hard to resist, but do you really need a "bigger" whirlpool tub? A "better" finish for the kitchen cabinets may not be really better, it may only be more expensive. A finish is a visual matter. Now, you may prefer a more expensive finish, but if you are already uneasy about escalating costs, select a less expensive choice. Two days after it's installed, you won't remember the other more-costly version.

Custom-made always means more money. If you can possibly live with a standard or stock item or finish, and cost is an issue, go that route. Doors and windows don't have to be the most expensive wood or be custom-made.

Electrical work often escalates, sometimes because of site conditions, other times because it makes sense to upgrade when you've got everything ripped apart. You always have choices and can say no, scale back, or choose a less expensive style.

Almost all large areas that need to be finished—walls, ceilings, and floors—are areas of potential cost escalation. Often it is the sheer number of square feet involved in these areas that tip the costs into big digit numbers. Try to get proposals or estimates for the work to be done in these areas as early in the project as you can. Once you have an idea of what flooring will cost, you can

RIGHT: One object can literally "make" a room. In this case, a magnificent, period, carved wood bed frame is the sum and essence of this bedroom—but don't tell that to the cat. *Design: Room Service Designs, Inc.; photo © 2008 by Phillip Ennis Photography.*

start your juggling act with the budget. Again, you always have choices, and your designer or any of the concerned contractors can be very helpful in guiding you into reasonable compromises.

Prices frequently get out of control with window treatments because most of the time you are dealing with custom-made items and sizable amounts of yardages. Make certain that you are comfortable with the designer's design, the workroom's work, and the pricing. If the installation does not meet your expectations, the options to make changes to the window treatment are limited and could prove to be costly.

Depending on how your revised budget comes along, try to squeak in an expensive fabric or two for the windows or upholstery. These are the areas that really show, and you want them to look as good as you possibly can.

Staying within Your Budget

In order to maintain control over the budget and avoid financial ruin, consider the following suggestions:

» Project a figure that will be your budget. Add 20 percent at the outset to make it more realistic.
» Decide the timing of your project.
» Allocate your funds into percentages based on the scope of work.
» Keep reviewing your documents and adding up the figures.
» Be aware of any rapidly climbing expenditure.
» Be prepared to make compromises (call them "executive decisions").
» If you have to, revise the early percentages. An allocation for construction 40 percent/furnishings 40 percent/accessories 20 percent may have to be changed to 50/40/10.
» Do not let one area move beyond a 10 percent change without sitting down and rethinking your objectives.
» Stop saying yes to changes, add-ons, and upgrades.

Project a figure that will be your budget. Add 20 percent at the outset to make it more realistic.

Seven

Everything is finally falling into place. Your major players have all been engaged, and the drawings and design are at a stage where the work can begin! Now what happens? Who shows up and when do they start?

Even when your project is a small one, it is your designer who will discuss with you what's involved, what procedures will take place, and who to expect on your doorstep. Your designer will provide you with the overall time frame of when things will happen.

Meeting before You Start

Any project involving contractors and one or more trades should begin with a thorough review of what is to happen. This should be a formally scheduled meeting and should include you, the designer, the architect, the structural engineer, and any other professionals involved such as the stone or painting contractors and the audiovisual consultant. In other words, anyone who is connected with your project in a major way should plan to attend. For very large projects the meeting is called the "pre-construction conference."

The pre-start meeting should cover everything that has to do with how your project is actually going to happen and what that entails. It prepares you for the days and months ahead. Be prepared to answer many questions concerning your household and how it will be affected during the time your project is being completed. You and your designer should use the following list to make sure that nothing is overlooked.

» **Daily schedule.** What will be the hours of operation? Will it be the same schedule every day or will it change according to the work performed?

» **Weekly schedule.** Is the schedule based on a five-day workweek? Will it change from week to week according to the work performed? Who will let you know?

» **Telephone use.** Is your house telephone available for calls or is it off-limits? Would you rather have everyone use their cell phones? If there is the equivalent of a job-site construction office, will a telephone be needed and will it require a telephone line? Do you have an emergency contact number? Who will collect and distribute a contact list of names and numbers of all people associated with the project?

» **Water use.** Will the work necessitate shutting off the water? Are all water lines affected? For how long? Will you be given temporary water connections? Are both hot and cold water affected?

FACING: A splendid solution to combine dining area, library, and countertop eating with lighting designed to serve all three functions. *Design: Room Service Designs, Inc.; photo © 2008 by Phillip Ennis Photography.*

» **Children and pets.** Are there children and/or pets in your household? Plan to keep the work areas off-limits to both. If either child or pet happens to get into a work area, have the work in the immediate area stopped, and have the child or pet escorted to a designated safe spot until you are contacted and can attend to their safety. Insist that the work crews notify you immediately if this happens.

» **Security.** Will someone have a set of your house keys for the duration of the project? Will it be only one person who has them and is responsible for them? Or will they be signed for and picked up and returned at the end of each day? Will you be giving out security keypad codes for entry? One idea might be to create a keypad code just for the project and change it back to your original code once the project is finished. Make sure that someone other than yourself knows how to shut off and reset your security alarm. If your alarm system rings right in the police station, advise your local authorities that you are having work done and to check with you or a designated contact person first before going out to check the premises.

» **Valuables.** Are there guns in the house? Jewelry? Money? Are they locked in specific protected devices? Would they be more secure if you were to move them to a different location? Do not leave anything valuable out or unprotected. If you have questions about what to do, ask your designer.

» **Protection.** How will your existing conditions and your possessions be protected? Make sure this is spelled out for you. Go over specific areas that will need special attention, such as wall papered walls, corners in a hall where sharp turns have to be made, sconces and chandeliers that can't be easily removed from walls and ceilings. These may need to be padded or wrapped, and power disconnected. The contractor will probably have you remove everything that could be even slightly in the way of the workmen. Carpeting and furniture need to be covered, as do stone surfaces (countertops and floors) and polished finishes (such as bathtubs and toilet seat covers). Anything where the gritty dust from a construction site can infiltrate and make contact with a surface needs to be protected. Dust is your number one enemy! Sometimes it's only surface damage, which can be dusted or washed away; other times it can create serious or permanent damage. Don't forget the areas outside the premises. Protect exterior landscaping, lawns, walkways, and driveway. Designate where people can walk and where deliveries can be made. These days many apartment buildings require the daily protection of floors and walls in the corridors. Your contractors and their crews will pay attention to your wishes, but you have to make them known.

» **Ventilation.** If there is a ventilation system in place and you intend to use it while work is being done, plan to have extra filters on hand and change them frequently. If weather and site conditions permit, try to keep the system off until you are through the construction phase. In the painting phase, your painters may or may not want the ventilation system on. The dust and particles generated by wall preparation are especially hard on a ventilation system. Again, if weather and site conditions permit, leave windows and doors open as much as possible. You will want to seal off all rooms where you will be spending time—bedrooms, kitchens, bathrooms.

» **Alternate facilities.** Will you need an interim kitchen or bathroom? If so, arrangements need to be worked out in advance. Review the planned arrangements with all parties concerned: designer/architect, contractor, plumber, and electrician.

» **Toilet use.** Work crews must have access to toilet facilities. If possible, designate one toilet in your home specifically for them to use.

Be prepared to answer many questions concerning your household and how it will be affected during the time your project is completed. . . . How will your existing conditions and your possessions be protected? Make sure this is all spelled out for you.

RIGHT: The inclusion of a library ladder in this home office makes the room at once interesting as well as practical. *Design: Favourite Finds; photo © 2008 by Hal Brown Photography.*

When the Work Begins

Some apartment buildings have toilet facilities that are available for workmen. But consider the value of time lost in making trips back and forth to the basement when making this decision. Depending on the job site and its size, you may have to rent a portable toilet.

» **Cleanup.** Decide who is to clean up the area each day. If you want the contractor to be responsible for this, it needs to be written into your contract, and the cost will be factored into the contractor's proposal. Find out whether the workmen will clean up after themselves or if a specific cleaner will be sent to do this. Ask when and how often he will come. As a money-saving measure, you may elect to clean up things yourself, but I don't recommend it. Designate a specific place where tools and buckets can be washed and a place to put the trash. Often a contractor provides a cleaning service to come in after the contractor's work is finished and thoroughly clean the project top to bottom. Your designer can make all these arrangements if your contractor does not.

» **Parking.** Will there be adequate space for the workmen to park? Depending on the size of your project and the type of work being done, there can be anywhere from one to thirty vehicles parked outside on a given day. Will your street or block accommodate a sizable influx of vehicles? Does your community have parking restrictions during the day? Do you need to notify the local authorities about this activity? Contact your neighbors and apologize in advance for the inconvenience they will undoubtedly experience.

» **Secure area.** The contractor will need to have an area set aside for the storage of tools, supplies, and equipment. Ideally, you want the area to be securely locked and held off-limits to anyone not connected with your project.

» **Insurance.** Arrange for a policy that covers your property, possessions, workpeople and their belongings, surrounding property, and anyone who is connected with your project for the period of construction and longer.

» **Point person.** One person on the contractor's staff needs to be designated as the "point or contact" person. Everyone involved with the project from you on down reports to this person. There may also be an equivalent person on the designer's staff. It is imperative that all information, news, changes, etc., be given to that one person. It is the only way to maintain control of the job.

Changing the Design and the Domino Effect

There is no way to avoid circumstances that require making changes to the design once the project is underway. That old scenario called "site conditions" reappears frequently. In addition to site conditions, changes in a product or its availability can alter the best-laid plans. Change is a fact of life, but having to make on-the-spot decisions is not. Ignore pressure tactics. There is no point in making a hasty decision you may later regret.

At this point in the progress of your project, most things have been decided and probably ordered. Each item has a place in the system; disturb one aspect, and, like a row of dominoes, one thing can adversely affect another.

I once designed a bathroom with a border of imported Italian glass tiles. I had spent a lot of time making sure that the border would meet the edge of the sink vanity counter, which had been custom-made for my tall clients. Then a well-meaning plumber asked me to either raise, lower, or shorten the border so it wouldn't interfere with the shower controls. He wanted a decision right then. I had him work on another part of the house while I studied the dilemma. In the end, the logical solution was for him to install the controls a little higher than normal, which put them above the border, and my tall clients were delighted with the decision.

Trying to find a solution that won't adversely impact adjacent parts is the goal. Things worked out well in this instance. But when they don't, look for the best compromise available. It may not make everybody happy—but that's what compromise is all about, isn't it? The bottom line is

Change is a fact of life, but having to make on-the-spot decisions is not. Ignore pressure tactics. There is no point in making a hasty decision you may later regret.

to get a solution that serves the best interests of all parties.

What about when decisions/changes are made when you are not around? At this point you probably trust your designer to make good decisions, but remember that it is your money and you must approve the change and preferably sign a change order (authorization form). Insist that your designer handle all changes by using a change order and insist on getting a price before you sign off on the change.

Sometimes an order may be delayed by a few months or unexpectedly discontinued, and a substitution has to be made. This is just the way business is today. Keep an open mind and you will find that things—no matter how bleak they may look at the time—always work out for the best.

Enjoying the Process

If you look upon this period as a great learning opportunity, you will get a lot of enjoyment out of the day-to-day process of completing your project. Plan to be around, not just to field questions as they come up but because your presence is important—to everyone. It is gratifying to be involved in a project where the client comes around and checks on the progress.

If you look upon this period as a great learning opportunity, you will get a lot of enjoyment out of the day-to-day process of completing your project.

You have a team working for you. Praise them when you are pleased. Treat the work crews to a freshly baked coffee cake every once in a while. Offer cold water, soft drinks, or hot coffee. You will get a lot of mileage out of a few simple acts of kindness.

Make sure you are reachable when you are not physically around, and be prompt in responding to any of the professionals who put out a call. Many times decisions do have to be made quickly, and since they always involve money and that involves you, any delays can be costly.

In the end, when the transformation is complete and the dust is gone, you will wonder where the time went. The commotion and smells will become distant memories, and you may even find yourself wondering if isn't time to tackle another project.

FACING: See how the cranberry walls in the room beyond the living room serve to punch up the palette of earth tones selected for the wall covering and furnishings. *Design: New York Interior Design, Inc.; photo © 2008 by Ivy D. Photography, Inc.*

Eight

The Project in Process

Lots of things take place during the course of a project as it evolves into a finished design. For you and the designer, this is the most exciting time of a project—when it's in process.

This is the period when the design comes to life before your eyes. There are strategies your designer can implement to minimize trouble spots. The following areas are things the designer can do to make a project run much more smoothly, even if problems can't be avoided entirely.

Site Meetings

Regular, planned site meetings are the best way to stay on top of a project. Consult with your designer on how this will be handled and if you are expected to attend. Use the list below as a cross-check for the designer's strategy:

» The meeting, which may often include all of the key players involved with your project, should follow a weekly schedule.
» An agenda should be distributed in advance, and it should include any concerns you, the client, have previously mentioned to your designer or contractor.
» Either the designer or the contractor is in charge of running the meeting: starting it on time, providing refreshments such as coffee and dessert, following the agenda, covering all the subjects on the agenda, and ending on time.

» Request that meeting minutes be taken, and that you get a copy.
» Raise any questions that you might have.

Who attends a site or construction meeting? The list should include, but is not limited to, any or all of the following:

» client
» architect
» interior designer
» general contractor
» project manager or site supervisor
» building superintendent
» lighting designer
» audiovisual consultant
» plumber
» electrician
» masonry installation foreman
» paint contractor
» cabinet shop supervisor

Holding site meetings is a sure way to maintain control over the schedule and uncover potential problems before they become real problems. Here is where you raise questions or express concerns about any aspect of your project. Someone in the meeting is certain to have a suggestion for what to do or who can resolve an issue. The meetings don't have to be weekly—that really depends on

FACING: Aged paneling gives the bar character and atmosphere and offers guests a warm welcome. *Design: Claudia Dowling Interiors; photo © 2008 by Ivy D. Photography, Inc.*

the size of the job—but, at the very least, they should be scheduled on a regular basis.

The Point Person

The point person, or "go-to" person, is the person to whom everyone reports, gives updated information, asks questions, or relays communications between offices, designers, and contractors. Usually the designer or the designer's second-in-command is the point person for the project. Sometimes on large-scale projects, there can be a point person assigned from each of the main offices—architect, interior designer, and general contractor—and they, in turn, communicate with one another.

This is, by far, the best way to manage a project. Your responsibility as the client is to communicate with the point person regarding any questions you may have, anything you want changed or that doesn't look right, or any topic you want added to the site meeting agenda.

Workroom and Workshop Visits

As the work on your project progresses, it becomes necessary to check on how things are going with the various products or services that are contracted for. Designers and architects make periodic stops at the workshops and workrooms. These trips are to review and check the work being done, to make decisions or course corrections, to resolve any questions or issues, and to see if the projected installation/delivery dates are on schedule. For the most part, the designer or architect makes these trips without the client.

At some point you might be asked to go to one of these workroom reviews, primarily the ones at the cabinet shop. When cabinetry components are partially assembled, when the basic shells have been constructed, one can then sense the size and look of the design. It's important for you

to experience this. It is at this point that you can begin to understand the scale of the unit first-hand and can see if the design is meeting your expectations. If a change needs to be made to the design, it will probably be for the better. Something as simple as reversing the swing of a door can make all the difference in how you will enjoy the completed unit. Be prepared to review the plans with the designer and make sure you like how it is being built.

A trip to the cabinet shop also gives you and designer the opportunity to finalize a custom finish or stain color. Of course, many clients don't have the time or interest in this day-to-day type of detail and leave this up to the designer. Whether you give approval by looking at samples or visiting the workshops, it is a process the designer can help you through.

Sometimes clients can visit drapery or upholstery workrooms with the designer, especially if they have particular concerns. Once window treatments are installed on the window, it is difficult—frequently impossible—to make changes after the fact, and it's always expensive.

Workrooms can always rig something up to illustrate the object in question. Whether it's a question of how a crown moulding will look on top of a wall unit or kitchen cabinet, what style to select, or how deep a valance should be, someone is always available to hold up something to simulate what it will look like.

Things are a little different with upholstery. Your designer will most likely want you to go to the upholstery shop and sit on the chair or sofa when it's covered in muslin—the last stage before the upholstery material is applied. If it doesn't feel terrific to you, then the fill of the cushions or the height of the arm or the pitch of the back must be adjusted. You have the opportunity to make that change with the designer at this point. Once the fabric goes on, it's too late. You may need to go in for a second "sitting" if alterations are needed. This is what "custom" is all about.

A designer makes sure you check out everything that needs your approval but won't usually take you shopping for fabrics or wall coverings. The choices available and the overall visual

stimulation is just too much for most people. Your designer already has a good idea of what will work for you and can cut through the shopping process much faster. And isn't that one reason you hired a designer, to refine the selection process? However, if you insist on looking for yourself, your designer will make arrangements to get you into the showrooms.

Client Availability

Most of the time clients are very amenable to adjusting their schedules to accommodate trips to a workshop. It is important, and often critical, in the timing of a project to get to the workroom when requested and finalize everything that is in question. If work cannot progress to the next

> Clients must communicate their schedules, needs, wishes, wants, and changes so that they are not the cause of further delays in a project.

RIGHT: A clever way of incorporating doorways and beams into shelving turns this tiny home office into a real storage center. *Design and photo © 2008 by Terry Stewart Interior Design.*

stage until a question or measurement is settled, the order is put aside, and the staff moves onto someone else's order on their list.

Economics drive the workrooms. When your order or project is put into the schedule of a workshop, it is given a time frame. An experienced shop will hold to the schedule, barring unforeseen problems. If the needed answers and decisions are not made in a timely fashion, the work ultimately is stopped. No one can afford to have people standing around. Once the order is stopped, it has to be removed from the area to allow the next order to be set up in its place.

If the work is halted, its projected finish date changes. This invariably impacts everything adjacent to where the item(s) is going. For example, if cabinetry is bumped back on the workroom's schedule, it could affect the scheduling of when you can have painting, wallpaper, floor coverings, or even window installations done. And those contractors aren't going to stand around either. They will also move on to the next project. So be prompt in responding to a workroom's queries.

The same issue happens at the job site with questions that constantly come up there. The client's presence is often needed on very short notice. If at all possible, try and be a part of the team and be at the job site as often as you can. Not only will you help keep things on schedule, but it boosts the morale of all who are connected with your project to know that what they are doing is important to you.

Decision Making

Of course, there are instances when a decision must wait for more information or for a response from the right person. Then everyone must wait. Take your time to get it right—sounds like a bit of a contradiction, doesn't it? Each and every decision carries with it far-reaching financial implications, so do not fall prey to pressure tactics from others, but be cognizant of the schedule your project must follow. Don't hesitate about being "the squeaky wheel" yourself; it's a tactic

that works. Insist that everyone on your team be responsive, and that includes you.

Delays

We have reached the unavoidable—the "D" word: delays. What can you do to avoid them? A failure to communicate information to the appropriate parties always seems to be the root of the problem. Sometimes it is a misinterpretation of information; other times it is incorrect information that causes delays. What can you to do to avoid them?

I was once creating a new bathroom for a client. The general contractor had not told her when he could start, so I didn't know when I was supposed to have the plans ready for him. I figured he would let me know well in advance, and we would meet and discuss it together. Two weeks before Christmas he suddenly announced that he was going to be at her house the next day to start work and did she have the plans ready for him? Well, of course she didn't and neither did I. I told her to be the squeaky wheel. No advance notice, it was the holidays—he needed to back off until the first of the year, which he did. And I had a chance to get the plans done. In this instance, the contractor unwittingly created the delay by not communicating his schedule. Communication is essential.

It's the same thing with orders. If a supplier communicates in advance that a product will be delayed, then there is time to make a substitution, reshop it, or reschedule other work.

Clients must communicate their schedules, needs, wishes, wants, and changes so that they are not the cause of further delays in a project.

Delays are simply inevitable. Products are mysteriously discontinued, furniture doesn't make it on the boat coming from the Far East, people get sick, someone in the family of a worker has a bad accident, the worker is off the job for a while—all kinds of unavoidable things take place when you have a big cast of people involved. Since you can't avoid delays, take them in stride. Tell yourself that's life and there will eventually be an end to the project.

Since you can't avoid delays, take them in stride. Tell yourself that's life and there will eventually be an end to the project.

Nine

After examining and reviewing ways to avoid or minimize problems that you may very well encounter during a design project, it boils down to this: too often, no matter how thorough the preparation of managing a project has been, no matter how much care has been taken by your design team, things just don't go right.

A lackluster performance on the part of a contractor, a big error in an order, inept workmanship on the part of an installer, or a clash in personalities may trigger the moment when it all falls apart. Tempers flare, threats and accusations are made, someone walks off the job. It happens. So what do you do when things suddenly are not going right?

Keeping Your Cool

Part of the problem is your proximity to the job site. You are there—where the action takes place. Try to keep your cool, no matter how incensed or upset you may be. As the client, you have every right to be upset, but telling someone off, threatening a lawsuit, or throwing someone off the job is not a cool way to handle things. What's more, you will always regret it later. If the situation has reached a level where it is really out of con-

trol, advise your point person immediately and address the issue with your designer.

I'm speaking here of a volatile, confrontational situation. What if the situation is one that is less specific? Perhaps it's a missing delivery, or you have a hard time reaching someone, or someone misses an appointment. Now you're disgusted. Days go by and your calls are not being returned. Now you're furious. Leaving menacing or threatening messages is a fast way to escalate a minor situation into a full-fledged disagreement. Don't do it. Advise your point person what has been happening and, again, address the issue with your designer.

You have one goal, one objective: to get your job finished. You must do whatever you have to do to get it done. Your designer knows how tough it can be to complete a project and how tough people can be to deal with. Your designer is used to handling tough situations and knows how to get things back on track. Work in partnership with your designer to create an effective procedure for dealing with a difficult situation.

FACING: A glorious interpretation of a contemporary dining room given real style with the introduction of antique American accessories and artifacts. *Design: Room Service Design, Inc.; photo © 2008 by Phillip Ennis Photography.*

Avoiding Problems

You want to avoid any possibility of your project being slowed down, undergoing costly delays, or having work stopped. Encouraging communication helps avoid problems that can lead to a serious dispute. Whether the difficulty is primarily between contractor and client, designer and contractor, client and designer, or all of the above, with no one communicating, you are at a dead end. Anytime communication stops, work stops.

What you want most of all is to avoid anything that would lead to litigation. You know that the road to litigation is paved with gold and that you have paid for the paving.

IF EVERYONE IS BEHAVING BADLY

Let's look at a worst-case scenario. You are not getting what you want, your patience has run out, and you have stopped making payments. Suppliers are refusing to deliver the goods. Or maybe it's the other way around, they are refusing to continue or finish the job, and you have stopped paying them. None of you are speaking. Any attempt at conversation quickly erupts into a shouting match. You are getting nowhere and are angry and upset.

The thought of firing everyone has occurred to you. As a designer, I am always aware how quickly any relationship that I have can turn during the course of a project. From vendors to salespeople to contractors, people (especially workpeople) seem overly sensitive these days and can often be temperamental.

What if it is your spouse or significant other who is acting unreasonably (rightly or wrongly) and starts making threats or refuses to make payments? What if demands are made that are difficult or impossible to fulfill? Well, if you value the relationship, and let's assume that you do, turn to the designer for help in negotiating an arrangement that will facilitate communication.

On the other hand, designers can behave badly, too. In addition to having outrageous, overblown egos and temper tantrums, they can make unreasonable demands, lie, or abscond with your

RIGHT: A lavish use of fabrics makes this dining room appear sumptuous and elegant; note the upholstered banquettes used for seating at both ends of the table. *Design: Michelle Wenitsky Interior Designs; photo © 2008 by Matt Wargo Photography.*

When Things Don't Go Right

money—or so I hear. If, by some serious stroke of bad luck, this happens to you, get legal advice as soon as possible to plan a course of action. Get all of your papers and documents pertaining to the project in order, as you will need to reference contracts, orders, and financial transactions.

Unfortunately, this is a business that fosters temperamental outbreaks because everything seems so critically important and life threatening. I frequently have to remind my staff (and myself) that I am not running an emergency room. I am running an interior design business. It helps to keep things in perspective.

Getting Things Back on Track

The approach to finding a solution for most problems is essentially the same. The designer, with your input, needs to first figure out what the problem is. If the problem surfaced on the job site, review what your first signals were that things were not going smoothly. That should give the designer a clue as to how the problem started and insight into what the problem really is.

Look at the way it escalated. Reexamine conversations and the pivotal moment when things started to deteriorate. With some hindsight, the seemingly unfathomable reasons for how this started begin to emerge and you see a chain of incidents that lead to where you are right now. The designer will use this insight to gain an edge in negotiating. You are looking for ways to convince someone to do something that at the moment they don't want to do.

When feelings are hurt, try kind words, a carefully phrased explanation of where you stand on the subject, and an apology to bring the person around. Apologize, even if you are apologizing on someone else's behalf; praise the person for what he does and say how much everyone needs him on the job—especially you. Commiserate by telling the person how hard he works, probably he's not getting enough rest, and what can you do to make things right?

When it's a question of money, agreeing to pay something usually works like magic. Offer an initial partial payment in return for an equivalent amount of work or a partial delivery. Will that be enough to get things going again? Assuming it is, and if that goes smoothly, then arrange for additional payments with similar incremental completions of work and deliveries.

If you have simply reached an impasse and no one is budging—this happens—my advice is to take a little time to get things worked out. Take a break from it all. Let some time go by. Often that's enough for one of the parties to see things in a different perspective (like wanting to be paid) and to agree to resume.

Sometimes it is wise to seek legal advice. Look for a lawyer who is familiar with the interior design and construction industries. Anyone knowledgeable who is in a position to look at the situation objectively is someone who can potentially give you advice. Often seeing a situation through someone else's eyes can be the turning point in how you assess a complicated state of affairs.

In the case where there has been a serious rupture in communication, and the designer or lawyer have been able to open the lines of communication, then a meeting needs to be called.

If you and your designer can get people to agree to a meeting, where everyone will be face-to-face around a table, then you most likely will be able to negotiate a working agreement.

Getting everyone to agree to discuss the situation is the hardest part. Once you have that in place, the designer will set forth the guidelines for the meeting in an agenda that will go out to everyone:

» No shouting or accusations will be tolerated.
» The designer will assign a "parliamentarian," someone who will make sure that any shouting or accusations will be stopped immediately, and whose role will be to keep everyone on course with the agenda and to maintain order.
» Each person is to bring whatever papers or documents they think necessary to illustrate their claim or back up their case.

When feelings are hurt, try kind words, a carefully phrased explanation of where you stand on the subject, and an apology to bring the person around.

RIGHT: One can retreat to a special corner in a pool house to escape sun and heat—designed to perfection in pure Moroccan style. *Design: Drake Design Associates; photo © 2008 by Eric Striffler Photography.*

When Things Don't Go Right

» Negotiation and compromise will be expected in order to obtain a solution.

» No one can leave the table until a solution has been found.

One idea for a solution might be to give a bonus or reward (financial or otherwise) if the person finishes what he promises to do sooner than when he says he will. Lots of people want more than anything to be rid of a situation, and an incentive to get finished even faster can be a powerful motivator.

In a case I heard about recently, a couple had contracted with a contractor to build an addition to their house. Halfway through the project, things became very ugly with the contractor; no work was done for several weeks; the contractor would not come back until more money was paid to him; the designer's attempts to intervene on behalf of the client were ignored; and the clients were unwilling to pay out more to someone as unreliable and threatening as this contractor was proving to be. Neither side was speaking to the other. Classic impasse.

The designer worked with her clients to set up a meeting with the contractor. They got the contractor to agree to meet with them. They promised the husband would not make threats or raise his voice at the meeting. They further agreed that they would be willing to pay the contractor more, but he had to agree to meet with them first. The payment would be held in escrow until the work was finished satisfactorily. But the money was there, and that way the contractor knew he would be paid.

At the meeting, since neither side wanted to continue working together, the contractor agreed to complete just the foundation work, which represented what they had paid so far in deposits, in an agreed time frame. If he did not meet the time frame, penalties would be incurred and deducted from the escrow account. If he finished early, he would be given a bonus equal to 10 percent of the escrow amount. In the end, all conditions were met, and, with the help of the designer, the clients went on to find another contractor with whom they are thrilled.

Managing Mates/Navigating Disagreements

The following are key issues where you must find ways to manage the differences if you and your mate are in disagreement.

DO YOU AND YOUR MATE HAVE A UNIFIED VOICE WHEN IT COMES TO THE DESIGN OF THE PROJECT?

Do not waste everyone else's time arguing about differences of opinion in a meeting. Explain why you prefer this and your mate prefers that, but let the designer try to figure out the best way to handle it. Compromises need to be worked out, and effort needs to be put into finding the areas where you both do agree. Do not argue in front of the work teams. It confuses people because they don't know which one of you to go to or whose opinion is the deciding one.

IF YOU DON'T AGREE, CAN YOU RECOGNIZE (AND RESPECT) THAT YOUR SIGNIFICANT OTHER IS ENTITLED TO A DIFFERENT OPINION?

Can you work out an arrangement whereby one of you says, "This is George's choice," and let the matter rest? Or, "We discussed this, and even though I think that is a better choice, Harold preferred this, and I want him to be happy." If you are really in opposition on an issue, look at it from the standpoint of which one of you will be spending the most time in the space—a home office or a kitchen, for example—and let that person's preferences prevail.

If it's a case of equal sharing of a bathroom, can you share design decisions as a form of compromise? "Okay, you can have blue tile, but I want individual sinks and a heated floor."

ARE BOTH OF YOU GOING TO BE INVOLVED IN THE DAY-TO-DAY DECISIONS AND MANAGEMENT OF THE PROJECT?

Usually I find one person of a couple is very engaged in the design process. The other gives opinions but seems to be very content to let the other person make decisions. If you both are committed as a team to your project, which I personally think is great, then act as a team. Discuss, resolve differences, and make decisions—it's very therapeutic. It will give you a closer relationship in the end, as you will have "built" something together.

THE PRINCIPAL PERSON

Is one of you the principal person who will deal with the workers, contractors, designers, architect, and deliveries? You both need to decide which one of you will be the point person for the designer and others to contact. There can't be two. Although your schedules may determine that Suzanne will be the point person on Tuesday and Wednesday and it will be Robert on Monday, Thursday, and Friday, make sure it is clear to everyone who is in charge. It does not mean the other person is excluded from the site or from the decision-making process; it just gives everyone a direct path to get questions and decisions addressed.

You may both feel more comfortable making decisions together. It's true, two heads are better than one and that way both of you know what is going on. But, logistically, it may be that only one person will be on-site when an immediate answer is needed for a question. Do you want to wait until the evening or whenever the other person is available to make a decision? Make the choice on how to and who will handle this at your pre-construction meeting. Do not wait until the first question comes up.

. . . Discuss a fallback position in case you decide to do more than you originally planned, or if you run into delays or other problems that could negatively impact your budget.

One way to handle this is to have one person do the daily troubleshooting and then give an update at the end of the day on the progress. Your mate may be really content to get a daily review and update. Again, make the decision early on which one of you will be designated to do this.

Are you agreed on the financial aspects of your project?

Have you both agreed on how your funds will be allocated: what percent to construction, what percent to furniture and furnishings, and what percent to finishing and accessorizing? Have you worked out together where the funds are coming from? Are you in agreement with what you plan to do if your funds run low?

First of all, come to an agreement on the budget and then determine where the funds will be used. You both need to agree on how much money goes where, and you both should be ready to compromise if you need to. It is so important to do this at the start of your project. Your preliminary decision isn't set in stone, so you can change your mind at any time, but it does give you and your spouse a starting point.

You also need to agree on where you will draw the monies from, especially if you are both contributing from different sources. Will your payouts be done on an incremental basis or on an "as needed" basis?

And most certainly discuss a fallback position in case you decide to do more than you originally planned, or if you run into delays or other problems that could negatively impact your budget.

Light at the End of the Tunnel

Whether your project is taking one month or a year or longer, there is always a moment when you feel it will never end, that the problems are relentless, that solutions are never found quickly enough, and that you wish you had never started it in the first place. Then one day, you will look around and it will occur to you that progress has been made. Perhaps you are ready for the painters, or the light fixtures are being installed, or the carpet is ready for delivery, and you will sense the first real taste of accomplishment. It is a delicious feeling.

This will give you the stamina and energy to forge ahead to the finish line.

When Things Don't Go Right

Ten
Completion and Closure

Now that you are nearing the completion of your project, you may have a different perspective of what has taken place during your job. Maybe you cannot wait for it all to be over, or maybe you realize that you are going to miss the day-to-day excitement of all the activity that an installation incurs. Most likely you are feeling a bit relieved and nostalgic.

The actual completion may be more of a trickle-down effect, or it might be an "opening night" blockbuster where you won't come in until it is all finished, the flowers are on the table, the music is playing, and the champagne is ready to pour. However, true closure does not happen until the last item on the punch list has been finalized and the last work person has left. It may seem like an endless process. Ultimately, however, the job is finished and you can start enjoying the changes to your life the new design has brought.

Making the Punch List

As the project nears completion, thoughts naturally turn to the punch list. A **punch list** is the term given to the document that the designer, architect, or contractor generates that is used to keep track of the many things on your project that need to be fixed or corrected in some way. Items on the punch list are referred to as being "open" until they are finished or "closed." Everything on the punch list must be completed or resolved before the project can officially be termed finished. For example, any item, piece, or part that is missing or is inoperable, is broken or bent, is unpainted or unfinished or in the wrong finish, is on backwards or upside down, or is chipped, nicked, scratched, dented, dinged, or damaged in some way is logged on the punch list.

Some clients will start their own punch lists as soon as items are delivered or installed, noting what is wrong. They go over their list with the contractor or the designer. As the client, you have the advantage of being able to immediately notice things that are wrong, since you are right there to see when something is not right or doesn't work.

Once all the work has been done, the designer, the contractor, and you walk through the project and develop the list. This is known as the "walk-through." The designer usually maintains the master list and coordinates what is on the list with the contractor. Once the list is written up, a copy is sent to you requesting that any errors, omissions, or additions to the list be brought to the designer's attention without delay. The designer

FACING: A cozy den where purple orchids on the coffee table spark the neutral tones of the textured wall covering and upholstery fabrics. *Design: Sheridan Interiors, Inc.; photo © 2008 by Wade Zimmerman, Photographer.*

Above: Accessories give this living room its stylistic punch: framed prints, sofa pillows, interesting objects on the coffee table, and a standing screen in the corner. *Design: Sheridan Interiors, Inc.; photo © 2008 by David Regen.*

and the contractor notify the party responsible for taking care of a particular item and review what action needs to be taken.

A punch list is usually organized by room or location and can be many pages long, depending on the size of the job. A designer might make up a sheet for each room and tape a copy to the wall, making it easy to see if an item is on the list or not. The punch list should contain the following information: the project name; date of the inspection/review; the room/location; the subject (electrical, plumbing, cabinetry, etc.); a brief description of what is wrong; the person, trade, or firm that is to make the correction; and the date the item is corrected or closed.

After the initial walkthrough and corrections are underway, expect the punch list to be reviewed on a regular basis by the designer and the contractor(s) until it is substantially completed. A wise designer will make sure that the client knows that the punch list items are being addressed as quickly as possible. This is a period when you may decide to withhold payments pending corrections. It is also the same period of time where getting workpeople to make prompt repairs, without payment of work done before, can be a delicate issue. Work with your designer to see which course of action is appropriate. Withholding payment is a leveraging tool that must be used prudently if it is to be effective. The designer knows how to work out side arrangements with people who do not respond promptly. A designer might have to make trades or deals in order to get the work done, but that is part of what you are paying them to do. Nothing leaves more of a negative impression in the mind of a client than a punch list that drags on and on.

Finishing the Finishing Touches

As many projects experience delays, getting to the finishing touches can be arduous. This is also the time in your life where you can be really tapped out—emotionally and financially. You don't want to make any more decisions or spend any more money. Understandable. Hopefully you have a designer who will support you through this period, otherwise you run the risk of becoming disinterested and never finishing the job.

This is the precise time when your project needs to look finished in order for you to experience a true feeling of satisfaction and closure. This will happen when the pictures are hung, tabletops have accessories, pillows are on the sofa, light fixtures have proper lampshades, and there are flowers in a vase. Nothing looks more unfinished than a room with just furniture, bare floors, and nothing on the windows.

Too often I have had clients stop just at this point—where everything has been delivered and installed but there are no accessories. Shop for accessories when you are buying furniture with your designer. It is easier to include purchases such as light fixtures and decorative accessories at this stage.

When you are out with your designer, talk about things for specific locations, such as a painting over the sofa. Watch for decorative artifacts that can be used in shelves and on coffee tables and credenzas. Frequently, when you spot something that really is a "find," the designer can determine right on the spot if it will fit into your space so you can make a very gratifying decision to buy it. Look at rugs on these shopping excursions, when you have furniture in the forefront of your thinking.

Listen to your designer when you are at the job site. Visual pictures are being planted in your mind by the designer when you hear how a certain wall needs a painting or how nice "that" will look once it has a few accessories on it. This is a good way to check if you are both on the same wavelength with the design direction the accessories will take.

If you need a break at the end of the design project, take it, but don't give up before you and your designer address the issue of accessorizing—only then will your project be truly finished. Be cautious about doing the accessorizing yourself. You may feel that you can pick out fabulous accessories and save yourself some money at the same time. Designers have spent years perfecting their eye

If you need a break at the end of the design project, take it, but don't give up before you and your designer address the issue of accessorizing—only then will your project be truly finished.

LEFT: Colorful accessories bring this sitting area to life. *Design: MH Studio LLC; photo © 2008 by John M. Hall Photographs.*

for selecting things that look good together. It is not difficult to tell a professionally designed room from one that is not, and the accessories are a true telling point.

If you don't have time to go shopping with your designer for accessories, there are several alternatives. Some clients prefer that the designer go shopping alone and surprise them. Some designers send images of items electronically to the client. If the client likes what has been selected, arrangements are made to send them to the job site.

If you are able to go shopping with your designer, several things can happen as you focus on the things that you both like. You can either purchase the items, put them on reserve, or take them out "on approval."

"On approval" means the client and/or the designer has the chance to actually see how something will look in the space. If it works and is approved by you, then it becomes an instant purchase and, happily, the item stays where it is. If it's not approved, it goes back to the vendor. Your designer will take things out on approval as much as possible. Not infrequently, measurements need to be rechecked or a color has to be revaluated. Most vendors will let you take things out on approval if a check or credit card is left to cover the total.

Want to know a terrific way to get your space finished with the designer basically doing all the legwork? Find out if your designer is planning to have your project photographed. The designer will bring in accessories, pictures, flower arrangements, maybe even a small table or two, or anything that is missing from the general scheme, for the photography. Remind the designer to keep the selections in a realistic price range—after all, you want to be in a position to buy these items.

The designer probably won't be returning things until the day after the shoot, and that not only gives you a chance to see how great everything looks, but it also gives you the time to think things over. It's to everyone's advantage to have you purchase as many items as possible. Not only will you get a dress rehearsal before making the commitment

to purchase, but you will have a fabulous-looking finished space with little effort. Some designers are more amenable to giving you a discount on the items they brought in because it saves them the time and money of returning them.

Staying in Touch: An Insurance Policy

After the project is finished, it's a good idea for you to stay in touch with your designer. You never know when something is going to get damaged or fail; and when that happens, you will want your designer to have repairs or replacements expedited. It's the best insurance policy for your investment.

The best way you can ever let your design team know that they have done a good job for you is to recommend your designer to any likely customers. Let your designer know when and to whom you have given referrals. This simple act will endear you forever to the designer.

Specialty Services

Most clients don't start another project for some time, but there are, in fact, several ways that a designer can continue to help a client. These are services that you may not realize a design office offers, but they are in areas that can prove very beneficial to you.

Nearly all interior designers offer what are called specialty services. Accessory acquisition is just one of those services. From a design standpoint, most designers include artwork with the accessories. Helping a client to hang their artwork correctly requires a trained eye. Be receptive to their expertise when it comes to hanging artwork.

In addition to hanging artwork and arranging accessories, your designer can offer you the following services in the area of entertaining:

The best way you can ever let your design team know that they have done a good job for you is to recommend your designer to any likely customers.

TABLEWARE AND ACCESSORIZING CONSULTATIONS

» Selecting and/or purchasing china, stemware, and flatware patterns
» Consulting on themes and table décor for the event
» Designing centerpieces and table décor
» Selecting table linens for a special event
» Creating and consulting on floral arrangements for the table and other locations
» Accessorizing the powder room with specially themed items for a party

SPECIAL EVENTS PLANNING

» Developing a theme for the event and a basic work plan for setting it up
» Coordinating colors, invitations, menus, seating, music, and table planning

» Working with a floral consultant for foliage and floral décor and other flower arrangements
» Finalizing wine and food selections, food preparation, party favors, beverage and food servers, coat checking, and guest seating
» Working and coordinating with a party consultant for large affairs

HOLIDAY PLANNING

» Making suggestions for decorating prominent areas and tabletops
» Suggesting unique or unusual ways of decorating or entertaining; creating a supplemental theme for the holiday itself
» Working out an entertaining plan for the holiday period, including menus
» Providing table decorations
» Decorating the Christmas tree and the social areas of your home

LEFT: To make a special occasion memorable, have a designer create the table arrangement and plan a menu especially for the event, such as the "Welcome Home" dinner pictured here. *Design: Sheridan Interiors, Inc.; photo © 2008 by Irving Solero.*

FLORAL ARRANGEMENTS

» Purchasing unique and creative floral arrangements for your special event
» Creatively using unusual combinations of colors and sizes of floral materials to match or accent your décor and make your event truly special

FUN PARTIES TO HOST

Consider giving a party for some different types of events. Your designer can help with any of the following:

» Formal tea party
» Wine tasting
» Desserts only
» Award winner or special achievement
» Birthday
» Graduation
» Shower: engagement, second time around, or baby
» Announcement: new job, first promotion, engagement, or marriage

» Three Kings Day
» Academy or Emmy Awards night
» Welcome home
» Retirement
» Summer or Winter Solstice/Spring or Fall Equinox
» House warming
» Halloween
» Valentine's Day
» St. Patrick's Day
» Farewell
» Bastille Day

Okay, It's Party Time!

The best way for a project to end is for you, the client, to have a housewarming party. It is also a great way to thank everyone involved with the project for a job well done.

Invite friends and family to show them how fabulous everything looks. Give thought to inviting the key players in the project—designer, architect, contractor, lighting designer, audiovisual consultant—anyone who played an effective role in its completion.

The stage is set to have a really glamorous evening. The designer will want to be there to make sure the flowers are fabulous, the lighting levels are set just right, the seat cushions and throw pillows are nicely puffed, the accessories are all in the right positions, and the food and beverage service are ready to go. The designer might even offer to share in some of the expenses since this is a beautiful opportunity to show off the project as well. An alternative idea might be to have a series of smaller, more intimate parties—if that's more your style.

Realize that your place will never look better than it does right now, when everything is fresh and newly installed, so you need to concentrate on getting this done. Besides, you'll tell yourself, the best reason to celebrate is because IT'S OVER!

I trust you now feel comfortable enough to use the services of an interior designer. Perhaps you will even embark on a design project that you have wanted to start for years. If you are already underway without a designer, you may rethink your approach and decide to engage one.

Wherever you are on the path of interior design, your journey is sure to have days that are uphill and some days where you coast along. There will be bumps and maybe a surprise pothole or two; you will experience twists and turns, lovely scenery, maybe a sudden downpour; but at the end you will come to a wonderful vista and, behold, there in front of you is where you live.

You can hardly wait to get home. You burst through the door at the end of day, and you come home to a design that is so welcoming, so comforting, so beautiful, so YOU.

FACING: Looking down on the seating area of a living room provides a full view of the accessories and the important role they play in design. *Design: Sheridan Interiors, Inc.; photo © 2008 by Wade Zimmerman, Photographer.*

The best way for a project to end is for you, the client, to have a housewarming party. It is also a great way to thank everyone involved with the project for a job well done.

Appendix

FACING: Here the designer has captured a feeling of dining in the French countryside by using a melange of French-styled furnishings and locating the table so that it takes full advantage of the windows and French doors. *Design: Michelle Wenitsky Interior Designs; photo © 2008 by Matt Wargo Photography.*

Sample Client Proposal Letter

May 20, 2008

Ms. Homeowner
105 Bayview Drive
Bronxville, New York 10543

Appendix

Dear Ms. Homeowner:

After meeting with you relating to the design and planning of your residence, it appears that we are ready to begin making definite plans.

This proposal is to generally outline our financial requirements with regard to our design services, responsibilities, and fees, as well as to define our role relating to other design professionals while we are engaged in this mutual collaboration. If you approve this proposal, then sign and send the initial payment, and we will submit a comprehensive letter of agreement.

Design Areas. Our work shall pertain to your entire residence. While you may retain an architect, and will hire a general contractor, our work shall be comprehensive to provide a complete design, harmonizing with the architectural plans based on our consultation.

Design Services. With respect to your entire residence, we shall perform the following services:

1 **Initial Design Study.** You have provided us with some existing floor plans that will most likely undergo revisions based upon your needs and requirements. Further consultation with you will clarify the scope of these revisions prior to the preparation of preliminary architectural and interior design concepts.

2 **Preliminary Interior Design Concepts.** A complete design presentation shall be prepared for your approval, summarized as follows:

 A **Drawings and Documentation.** We will detail all interior changes for your renovation.
 B **Preparation of Complete Floor Plans.** These will be drawn to scale and will include a proposed furniture layout.
 C **Finalization of All Working Drawings.** Subsequent to initial preparation, all working drawings will be submitted for your design professionals involved with your project. Any necessary revisions will be made, and final approval will be acknowledged by you in writing.
 D **Preliminary Design Concepts.** Upon your approval of our layout drawings, our complete presentation shall include furniture selections, materials (fabrics, wall coverings, window treatments, floor coverings, color schemes, lighting, etc.) and other visual aids necessary to illustrate our design plan.

Purchases. All purchases will be made available to you at the wholesale or net price of the item or service. We will act as your purchasing agent and all invoices from vendors will be forwarded to our office for payment. We will prepare all specifications and purchase orders, which shall specify payment terms that you must comply with, but we will deal with the vendors on a financial basis.

Compensation. Our office will bill on an hourly basis for our design, shopping, and planning services as specified by the description of our design services.

Rates are scheduled as follows:

> Principal of firm - $____._ per hour
> Senior designer - $____._ per hour
> Drawing/drafting - $____._ per hour

Further, the fees for selecting and specifying all purchases as well as services provided through this office shall be based on _____ percent (__%) above the wholesale or net price of the item or service.

If the above meets with your approval, your signature below will indicate your acceptance of the basic terms of our agreement. Kindly return one signed copy to this office together with the initial payment of $_____._, which represents a retainer to be credited against hourly billing; you will be sent a more detailed letter of agreement within a few weeks. Of course, if you have any questions, don't hesitate to call.

We look forward to working with you on your lovely new residence.

Sincerely yours,

_____
Name of Designer

_____
Name of Firm

ACCEPTED: _____ Date _____
          (Signature of Client)

Sample Client Acceptance Letter

May 20, 2008

Dr. & Mrs. Homeowner
1025 Park Avenue
New York, New York 10021

Dear Henry and Linda:

Thank you very much for contacting me with regard to the proposed decorating of your residence at the above address. I am so pleased that you found me through _____ and I look forward to a rewarding, collaborative association with you. As I mentioned on _____, my customary procedure in starting a project is to submit an acceptance letter, which serves to define our roles for the current working relationship.

Based on the information that we reviewed, what I propose for the financial arrangements concerning the services required for the design and finishing details of the following areas is as follows:

Living/Dining/Entry Area
Den/Guest Bedroom
Kitchen/Breakfast Room
Bathroom
Master Bedroom

1 Design Concept Services:

» Determine your design preferences and requirements.
» Conduct a design study, including photographing and measuring the aforementioned areas (only as required).
» Prepare furniture floor plans and drawings as needed and provide any materials necessary to present proposed design concepts.
» As required, shop and select items from showrooms, retail stores, or catalogues at your directive.
» Provide suggestions, guidance, and expertise with regard to any area requiring design solutions, including an estimated budget.

2 Project Review:

» Conduct reviews in cabinet shops, drapery/upholstery workrooms, or workshops.
» Hold meetings or reviews with you, including your consultants, agents, contractors, workmen, installers, or staff at the project site, my office or theirs, or by telephone.

3 Purchasing Services:

» Determine merchandise and installation services to be purchased through me and specified in a written proposal.

» Merchandise and services, including custom designed items and furniture, *will be billed to you at the net cost of the item or service, plus a 20% administration fee*. No order will be processed until your written approval and initial payment have been returned to me.
» The proposal will require a 50 percent deposit and your signature.
» Proposals for in-stock items such as fabrics, wall coverings, accessories, antiques, and items purchased at auction or in retail stores will be issued as invoices and will require full payment upon submission.

Additionally, all disbursements related to the project, such as blueprinting, film and developing, messenger/express delivery, toll telephone/fax, travel/transportation expenses, and other out-of-pocket expenses will be billed separately.

The design firm of _____ shall be compensated for design concept services on an hourly basis at the rate of $_____ per hour, billed in 15-minute increments. When travel outside _____ is required for services as noted above, time spent en route will be billed separately at $_____ per hour in 15-minute increments. Hourly charges will be invoiced to you monthly and are payable by you upon receipt of invoice.

Upon signing this agreement, the design firm shall receive a nonrefundable initial advance of _____ (write out in words) _____ dollars ($____.__), which constitutes the minimum fee due designer for design concept services. This advance will be credited against hourly charges otherwise payable by you to the design firm for design concept services, and will be submitted as an invoice when the project nears completion.

To signify your acceptance of our working arrangement, please sign this letter where indicated. Return it to my office, together with a check in the amount of $____.__, which represents full payment of the advance.

I am truly looking forward to working with you both on your charming apartment.

Best regards,

_____
Name of Designer

ACCEPTED: _____   Date _____
          (Signature of Client)

ASID Document 124
Residential Interior Design Services Agreement

Special Instructions Regarding Page 2

Note that this Agreement contains two alternative paragraphs 1.2. Each alternative appears on a separate "Page 2." Except for Paragraph 1.2, the remaining language on each alternative "Page 2" is identical.

If Designer intends to charge a fixed fee for Design Concept Services, then (1) carefully remove and discard the second "Page 2"; and (2) use the first "Page 2" which contains the following language in Paragraph 1.2:

> *Prior to commencing Design Concept Services, Designer shall receive an Initial Design Fee of _____ dollars ($_____). This non-refundable Design Fee is payable upon singing this Agreement and is in addition to all other compensation payable to Designer under this Agreement. Not more than _____ (___) revisions to the Design Concept will be prepared by Designer without additional charges. Additional revisions will be billed to Client as Additional Services.*

If Designer intends to charge hourly fees for Design Concept Services, then (1) carefully remove and discard the first "Page 2"; and (2) use the second "Page 2" which contains the following language in Paragraph 1.2:

> *Designer shall be compensated for its Design Concept Services on an hourly basis at the rates set forth in paragraph 4.1 of this Agreement. Hourly charges will be invoiced to Client _____ and are payable by Client upon receipt of invoice. Upon signing this Agreement, Designer shall receive a non-refundable initial advance of _____dollars ($_____), which constitutes the minimum fee due Designer for Design Concept Services. This advance will be credited against hourly charges otherwise payable by Client to Designer for Design Concept Services.*

ID124-1996

ASID Document ID124
Residential Interior Design Services Agreement

This **agreement** is made this _____ day of _____ in the year of Two Thousand and _____

Between the **Client**:
(name and address)

and the **Designer**:
(name and address)

The **Client** and the **Designer** agree as follows:

The Project pertains to the following areas within Client's residence located at
_____ :

(List areas below:)

ID124-1996 1

Interior Design Services

1. Design Concept Services

1.1 In this phase of the Project, Designer shall, as and where appropriate, perform the following:

    A. Determine Client's design preferences and requirements.

    B. Conduct an initial design study.

    C. Prepare drawings and other materials to generally illustrate Designer's suggested interior design concepts, to include color schemes, interior finishes, wall coverings, floor coverings, ceiling treatments, lighting treatments and window treatments.

    D. Prepare layout showing location of movable furniture and furnishings.

    E. Prepare schematic plans for recommended cabinet work, interior built-ins and other interior decorative details ("Interior Installations").

1.2 Prior to commencing Design Concept Services, Designer shall receive an Initial Design Fee of _____ dollars ($___). This non-refundable Design Fee is payable upon signing this Agreement and is in addition to all other compensation payable to the Designer under this Agreement. Not more than _____ (___) revisions to the Design Concept will be prepared by Designer without additional charges. Additional revisions will be billed to Client as Additional Services.

2. Interior Specifications and Purchasing Services

2.1 Upon Client's approval of the Design Concepts, Designer will, as and where appropriate:

    A. Select and/or specially design required Interior Installations and all required items of movable furniture, furnishings, light fixtures, hardware, fixtures, accessories and the like ("Merchandise").

    B. Prepare and submit for Client's approval Proposals for completion of Interior Installations and purchase of Merchandise.

2.2 Merchandise and Interior Installations specified by Designer shall, if Client wishes to purchase them, be purchased solely through Designer. Designer may, at times, request Client to engage others to provide Interior Installations, pursuant to the arrangements set forth in the Project Review services described in paragraph 3 of this Agreement.

ID124-1996 2

Interior Design Services

1. Design Concept Services

1.1 In this phase of the Project, Designer shall, as and where appropriate, perform the following:
  A. Determine Client's design preferences and requirements.
  B. Conduct an initial design study.
  C. Prepare drawings and other materials to generally illustrate Designer's suggested interior design concepts, to include color schemes, interior finishes, wall coverings, floor coverings, ceiling treatments, lighting treatments and window treatments.
  D. Prepare layout showing location of movable furniture and furnishings.
  E. Prepare schematic plans for recommended cabinet work, interior built-ins and other interior decorative details ("Interior Installations").

1.2 Designer shall be compensated for its Design Concept Services on an hourly basis at the rates set forth in paragraph 4.1 of this Agreement. Hourly charges will be invoiced to Client _____ and are payable by Client upon receipt of invoice. Upon signing this Agreement, Designer shall receive a non-refundable initial advance of _____dollars ($____), which constitutes the minimum fee due Designer for Design Concept Services. This advance will be credited against hourly charges otherwise payable by Client to Designer for Design Concept Services.

2. Interior Specifications and Purchasing Services

2.1 Upon Client's approval of the Design Concepts, Designer will, as and where appropriate:

A. Select and/or specially design required Interior Installations and all required items of movable furniture, furnishings, light fixtures, hardware, fixtures, accessories and the like ("Merchandise").

B. Prepare and submit for Client's approval Proposals for completion of Interior Installations and purchase of Merchandise.

2.2 Merchandise and Interior Installations specified by Designer shall, if Client wishes to purchase them, be purchased solely through Designer. Designer may, at times, request Client to engage others to provide Interior Installations, pursuant to the arrangements set forth in the Project Review services described in paragraph 3 of this Agreement.

ID124-1996 2

2.3 Merchandise and Interior Installations to be purchased through Designer will be specified in a written "Proposal" prepared by Designer and submitted in each instance for Client's written approval. Each Proposal will describe the item and its price to Client (F.O.B. point of origin). The price of each item to Client ("Client Price") shall be the amount charged to Designer by the supplier of such item ("Supplier Price"), plus Designer's fee equal to _____ percent (____%) of the Supplier Price (exclusive of any freight, delivery or like charges or applicable tax).

2.4 No item can be ordered by Designer until the Proposal has been approved by Client, in writing, and returned to Designer with Designer's required initial payment equal to _____ percent (____%) of the Client Price. The balance of the Client Price, together with delivery, shipping, handling charges and applicable taxes, is payable when the item is ready for delivery to and/or installation at Client's residence, or to a subsequent supplier for further work upon rendition of Designer's invoice. Proposals for fabrics, wall coverings, accessories, antiques, and items purchased at auction or at retail stores require full payment at time of signed Proposal.

3. Project Review

3.1 If the nature of the Project requires engagement by Client of any contractors to perform work based upon Designer's concepts, drawings or interior design specifications not otherwise provided for in the Interior Specifications and Purchasing Services, Client will enter into contracts directly with the concerned contractor.

3.2 Designer will make periodic visits to the Project site as Designer may consider appropriate to observe the work of these contractors to determine whether the contractor's work is proceeding in general conformity with Designer's concepts. Constant observation of work at the Project site is not a part of Designer's duties. Designer is not responsible for the performance, quality, timely completion or delivery of any work, materials or equipment furnished by contractors pursuant to direct contracts with Client.

3.3 Time expended by Designer for all Project Review services will be charged to Client on an hourly basis at the rates set forth in paragraph 4.1 of this agreement.

4. MISCELLANEOUS

4.1 Should Designer agree to perform any design service not described above, such "Additional Service" will be invoiced to Client at the following hourly rates:

Design Principal	$_____
Project Designer	$_____
Staff Designer	$_____
Draftsman	$_____
Other employees	$_____

Hourly charges will be invoiced to Client _____ and are payable upon receipt of invoice.

ID124-1996 3

4.2 Disbursements incurred by Designer in the interest of the Project shall be reimbursed by Client to Designer upon receipt of Designer's invoices, which are rendered _____. Reimbursements shall include, among other things, costs of local and long distance travel, long distance telephone calls, duplication of plans, drawings and specifications, messenger services and the like.

4.3 Designer's drawings and specifications are conceptual in nature and intended to set forth design intent only. They are not to be used for architectural or engineering purposes. Designer does not provide architectural or engineering services.

4.4 Designer's services shall not include undertaking any responsibility for the design or modification of the design of any structural, heating, air-conditioning, plumbing, electrical, ventilation or other mechanical systems installed or to be installed at the Project.

4.5 Should the nature of Designer's design concepts require the services of any other design professional, such professional shall be engaged directly by Client pursuant to separate agreement as may be mutually acceptable to Client and such other design professional.

4.6 As Designer requires a record of Designer's design projects, Client will permit Designer or Designer's representatives to photograph the Project upon completion of the Project. Designer will be entitled to use photographs for Designer's business purposes but shall not disclose Project location or Client's name without Client's prior written consent.

4.7 All concepts, drawings and specifications prepared by Designer's firm ("Project Documents") and all copyrights and other proprietary rights applicable thereto remain at all times Designer's property. Project Documents may not be used by Client for any purpose other than completion of Project by Designer.

4.8 Designer cannot guarantee that actual prices for merchandise and/or interior installations or other costs or services as presented to Client will not vary either by item or in the aggregate from any Client proposed budget.

4.9 This Agreement may be terminated by either party upon the other party's default in performance, provided that termination may not be effected unless written notice specifying nature and extent of default is give to the concerned party and such party fails to cure such default in performance within _____ (____) days from date of receipt of such notice. Termination shall be without prejudice to any and all other rights and remedies of Designer, and Client shall remain liable for all outstanding obligations owed by Client to Designer and for all items of merchandise, interior installations and other services on order as of the termination date.

4.10 In addition to all other legal rights, Designer shall be entitled to withhold delivery of any item of merchandise or the further performance of interior installation or any other services, should Client fail to timely many any payments due Designer.

ID124-1996 4

4.11 Any controversy or claim arising out of or relating to this Agreement, or the breach thereof, shall be decided by arbitration only in the _____ in accordance with the Commercial Arbitration Rules of the American Arbitration Association then in effect, and judgment upon the award rendered by the arbitrator(s) may be entered in any court having jurisdiction thereof.

4.12 Client will provide Designer with access to the Project and all information Designer may need to complete the Project. It is Client's responsibility to obtain all approvals required by any governmental agency or otherwise in connection with this Project.

4.13 Any sales tax applicable to Design Fees, and/or merchandise purchased from Designer, and/or interior installations completed by Designer shall be the responsibility of Client.

4.14 Neither Client nor Designer may assign their respective interests in this Agreement without the written consent of the other.

4.15 The laws of the State of _____ shall govern this Agreement.

4.16 Any provision of this Agreement held to be void or unenforceable under any law shall be deemed stricken, and all remaining provisions shall continue to be valid and binding upon both Designer and Client.

4.17 This Agreement is a complete statement of Designer's and Client's understanding. No representations or agreements have been made other than those contained in this Agreement. This Agreement can be modified only by a writing signed by both Designer and Client.

ID124-1996 5

5.   Additional Terms

Client: _____

_____

Designer: _____

_____

ID124-1996 6

Sample Proposal Letter

To: Mr. and Mrs. Homeowner
1133 White Plains Road
Hartsdale, NY 12345

March 9, 2008
Page 1 of 1

Re: Project Code: 09865

Quantity	Description	Unit Price	Extended Price
Master Bedroom			
1	All-upholstered Bridgewater armchair, with loose seat and back cushions, down wrapped dacron fill; waterfall front skirt with a pleated side panel design. Dimensions: 33" wide, 39" deep, 36" back height, 23" arm height, 19" seat height. *Ref. #: 0251*	 1,837.08	1,837.08
1	Companion ottoman, with an attached seat cushion, waterfall skirt with side pleats. Dimensions: 23" x 28" x 18" high *Ref. #: 0252*	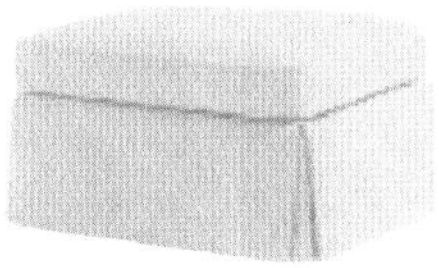 907.20	907.20

Item Total	2,744.28
Administrative Fee	548.86
Sales Tax	226.40
Grand Total	3,519.54
Requested Deposit	$1,646.57

Designer _____ Date _____

Approved _____ Date _____

Sample Sketch of Kitchen found on

pages 65 and 66

Utility Cl. Pantry Ref.

T. Stewart "05"

List of Interior Design Services

We provide:

» Measuring
» Drafting and drawing
» Elevations
» Floor plans
» Photography
» Preconstruction meeting with client, contractor, and designer
» Coordinating and scheduling all work
» Overseeing work in progress
» Post-construction reviews, punch lists, and final sign-off
» Guidance in selecting artwork
» Improvements for existing conditions

We design:

» Furniture layouts and space planning
» Room arrangements
» Closet interiors
» Color schemes and finishes
» Custom furniture
» Bed treatments
» Window treatments
» Cabinetry and built-ins
» Lighting plans
» Wall treatments: special finishes, wall coverings, wall upholstery
» Custom lampshades
» Wall arrangements: picture framing, hanging, placing artwork

We supply:

» Client presentations
» Estimates
» A budget
» Audio/visual system upgrades
» Electrical improvements and upgrading
» Kitchen design and renovation
» Bathroom design and renovation
» Answers to almost anything you ask
» Maintenance and repair tips
» Solutions to problems, informed opinions, and cleaning tips
» A batch of homemade biscotti (or cookies, if you prefer)

We offer:

» Full-scale renovations
» Accessorizing
» Shopping and selection of fabrics, furniture, and antiques, locally and abroad
» Furniture refinishing, polishing, replating, and repairing
» Restoration of floors, paneling, furniture, plasterwork, and antiques
» Exclusive trimming and upholstery techniques
» Customized linens and bedding
» Reuse/refurbishing of your existing furnishings
» Turnkey installations

LEFT: Inspired by the colors in the bed pillow fabric, the window curtains and wall color give special meaning to a guest bedroom. *Design: Michelle Wenitsky Interior Design; photo © 2008 by John Welsh Photography.*

INTERIOR DESIGNERS
*Featured in the book

Atkinson + Design, Inc.*, 32
458 Gerrand Street East
Toronto, Ontario, Canada M5A 2H3
416·920·9030
http://www.atkinsonplusdesign.ca

The Baltimore Design Center*, 36, 37
35 Main Street
Port Washington, NY 11050
516·944·2400
www.baltimoredesigncenter.com

Baron·Goldstein Design Associates
Roslyn, NY
516·627·8604
www.barongoldsteindesign.com

Bartlett & Associates, LTD
2A Gibson Avenue
Toronto, Ontario, Canada M5R 1T5
416·926·8247

Charles Pavarini III Design Associates, Inc.
243 West 98th Street, Studio #7-D
New York City, NY 10025
212·749·2047
www.pavarinidesign.com

Charm & Whimsy
143 Madison Avenue
New York City, NY 10016
212·683·7609
www.charmandwhimsy.com

Claudia Dowling Interiors*, 9, 92
325 Main Street
Huntington, NY 11743
631·421·5290
www.claudiadowlinginteriors.com

Colleen Grace Designs*, 44, 73
34 Andover Road
Hartsdale, NY 10530
914·949·1975
colleengracedesigns@msn.com

Design Concepts Interiors, LLC
8 Devonshire Court
Cortlandt Manor, NY 10567
914·734·1383
www.designconceptsinteriors.com

DCA Design Inc*, 19, 57, 133
220 Avenue Road
Toronto, Ontario, Canada M5R 2J4
416·531·8155 ext. 27
www.dcadesign.ca

Dodds & Eder*, 31
221 South Street
Oyster Bay, NY 11771
516·922·4412
www.doddsandeder.com

FACING: The dark surround
of shutters and shelves
gives this library/den a cozy,
intimate quality—so right for
sharing a drink in front of the
fireplace. *Design: DCA Design
Inc; photo © 2008 by Michael
Mahovlich Photography.*

133